AF478847

beelden aan zee museum

Architect Wim Quist

beelden

museum

Contents

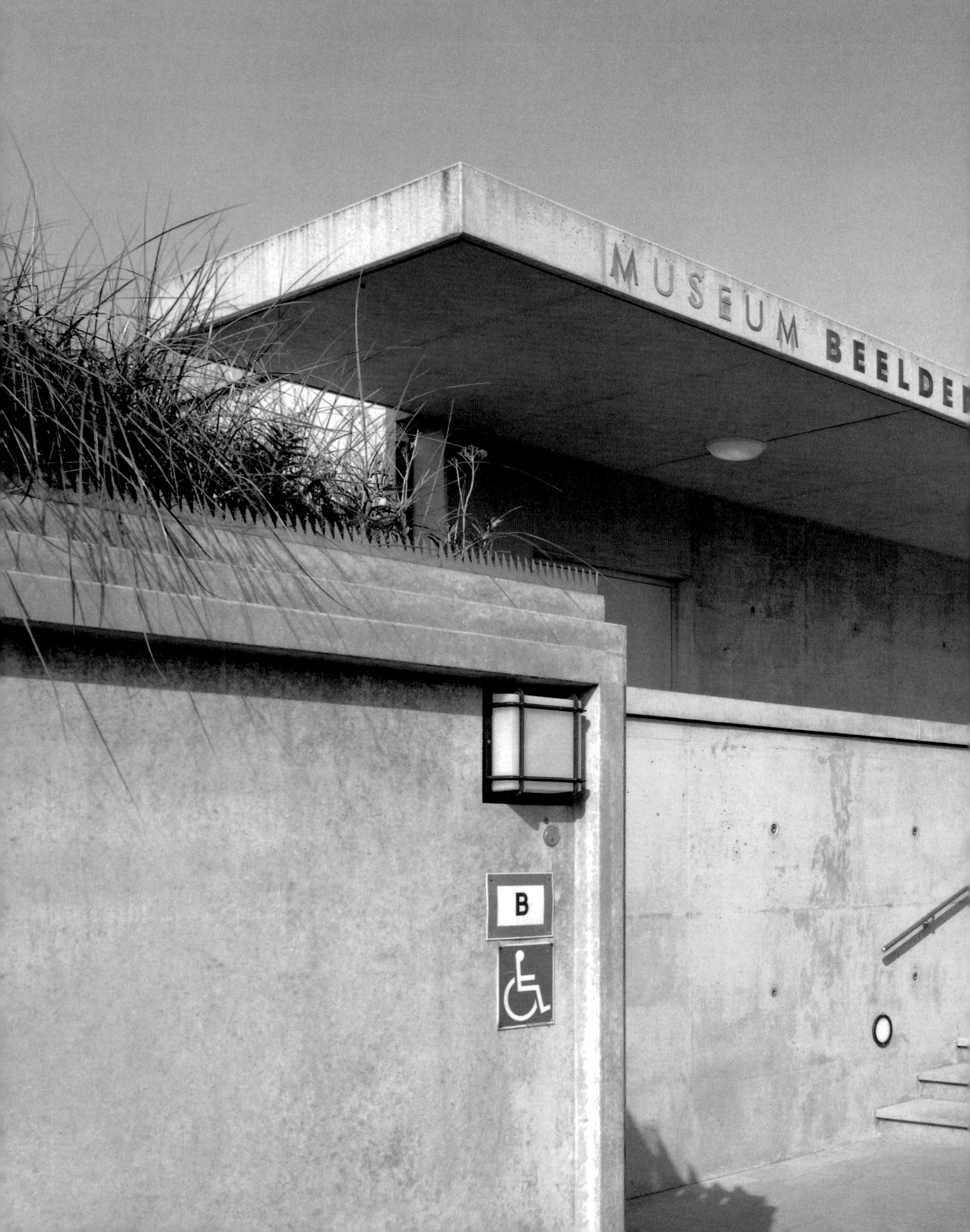

MUSEUM BEELDEN
B

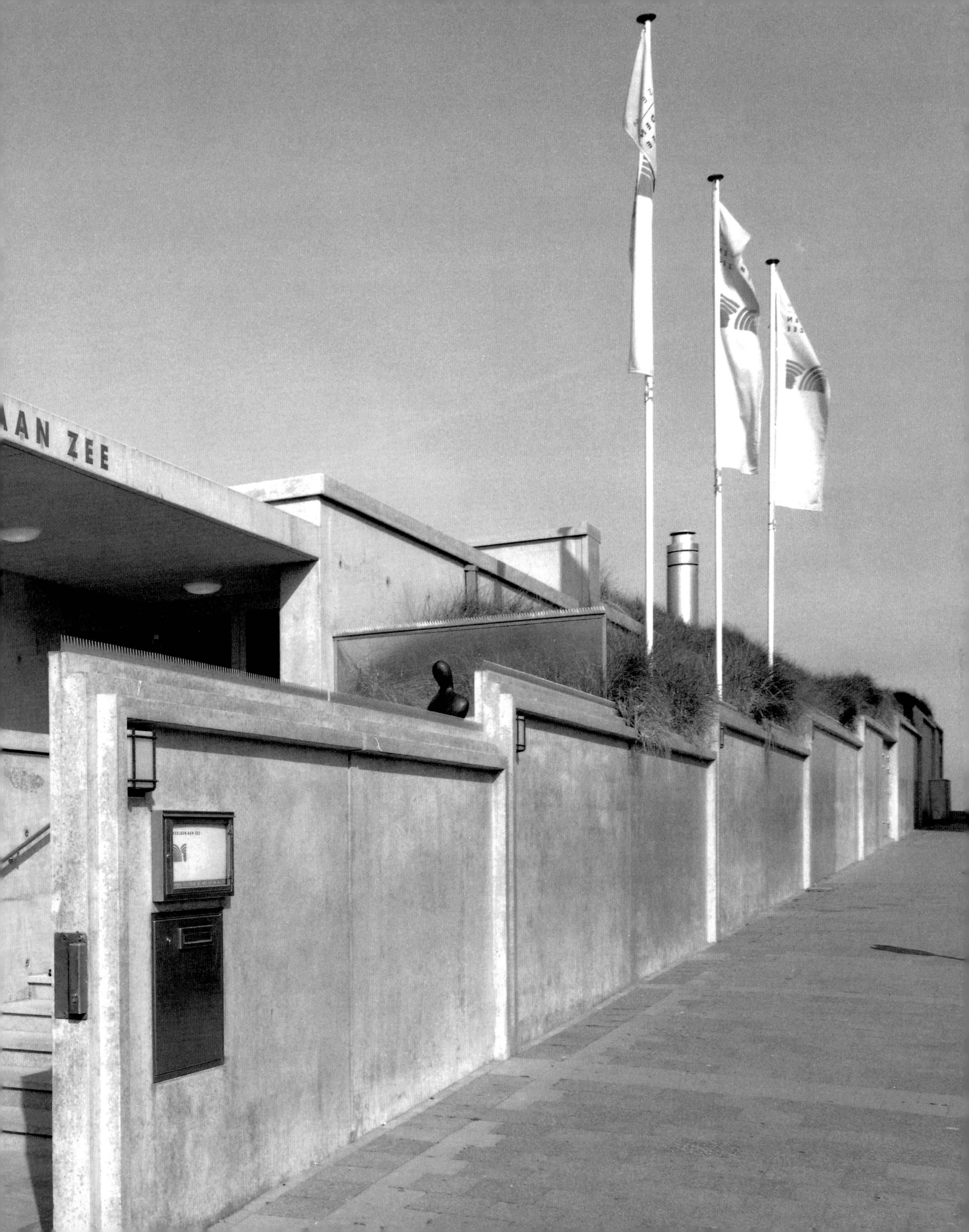

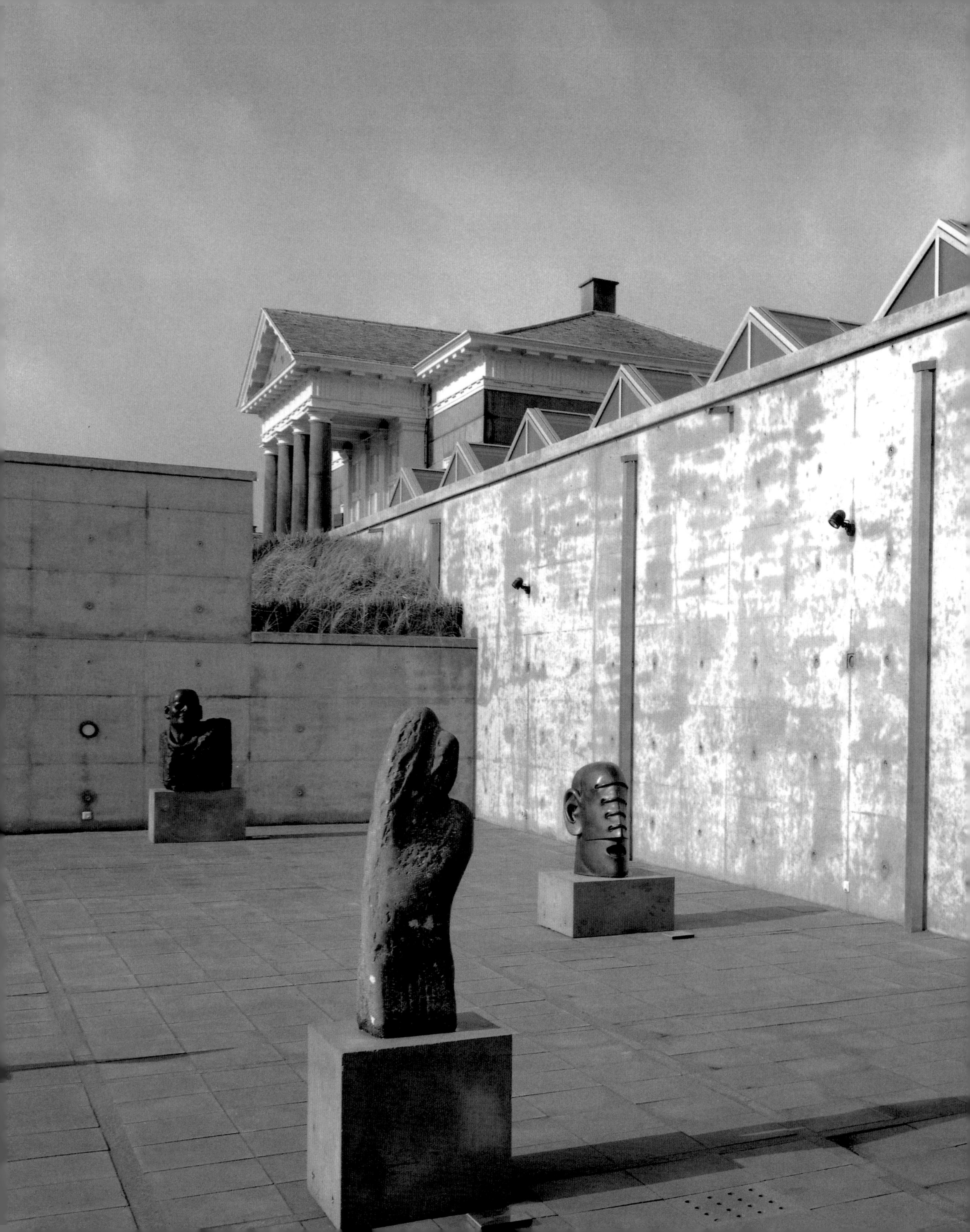

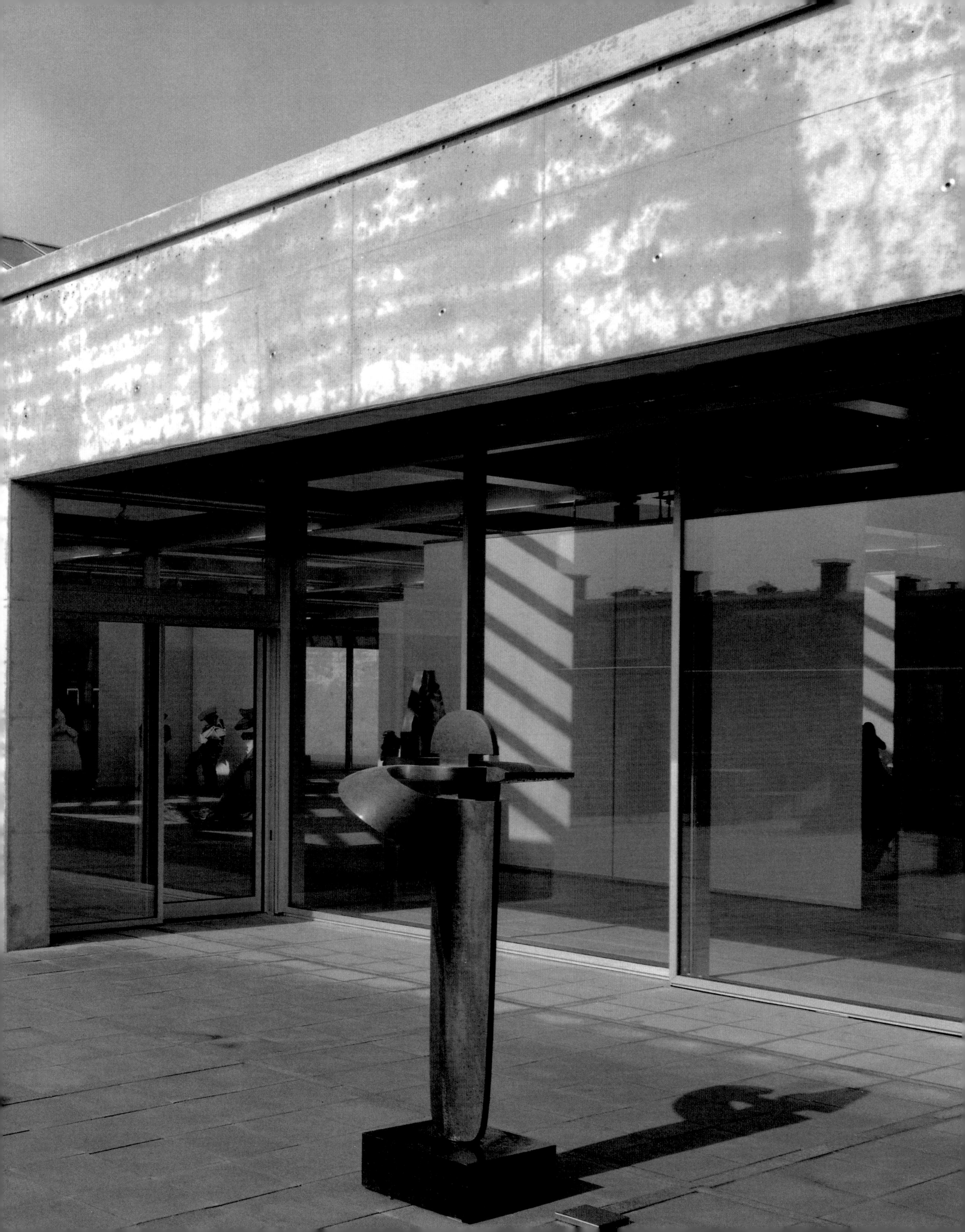

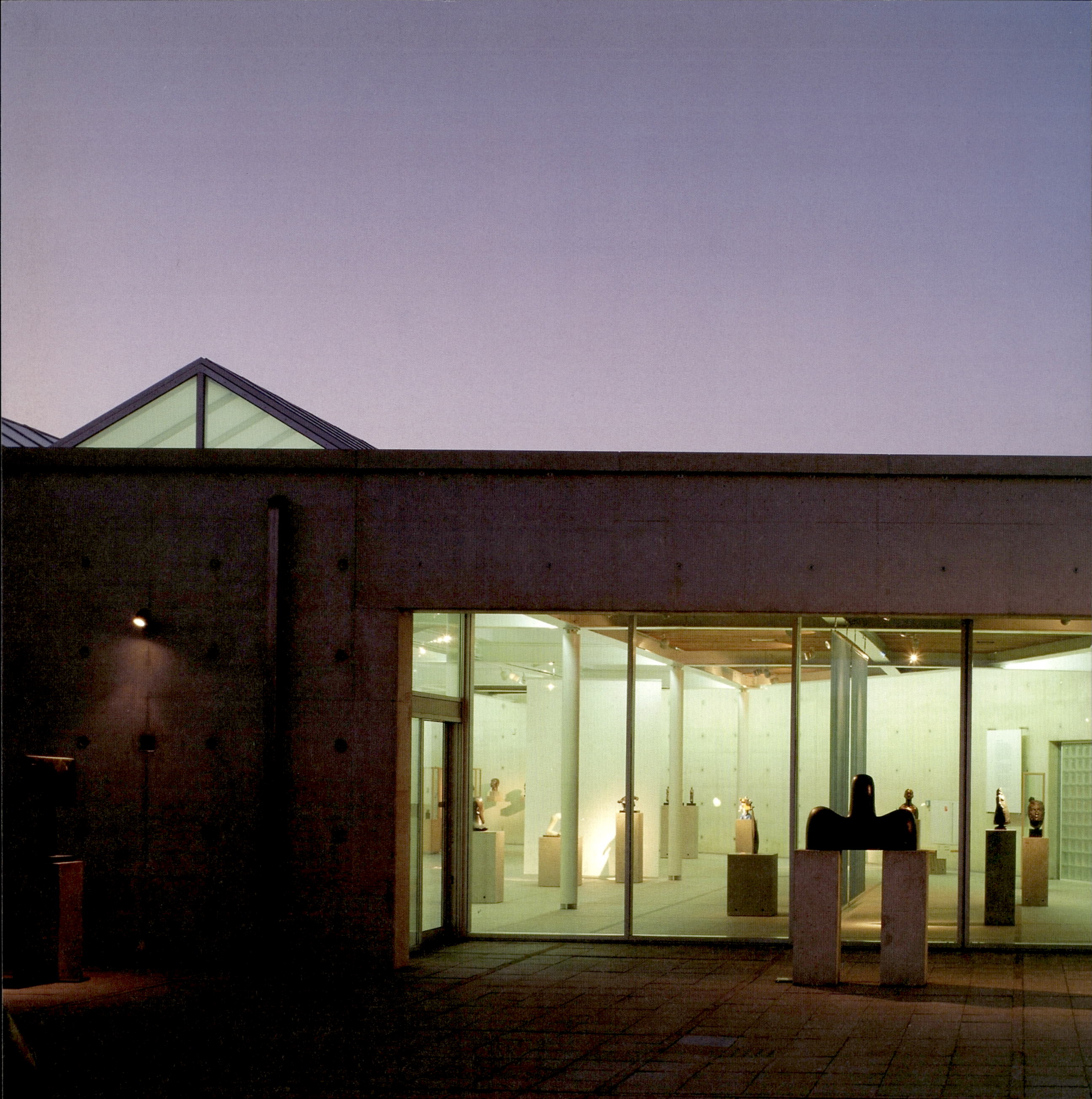

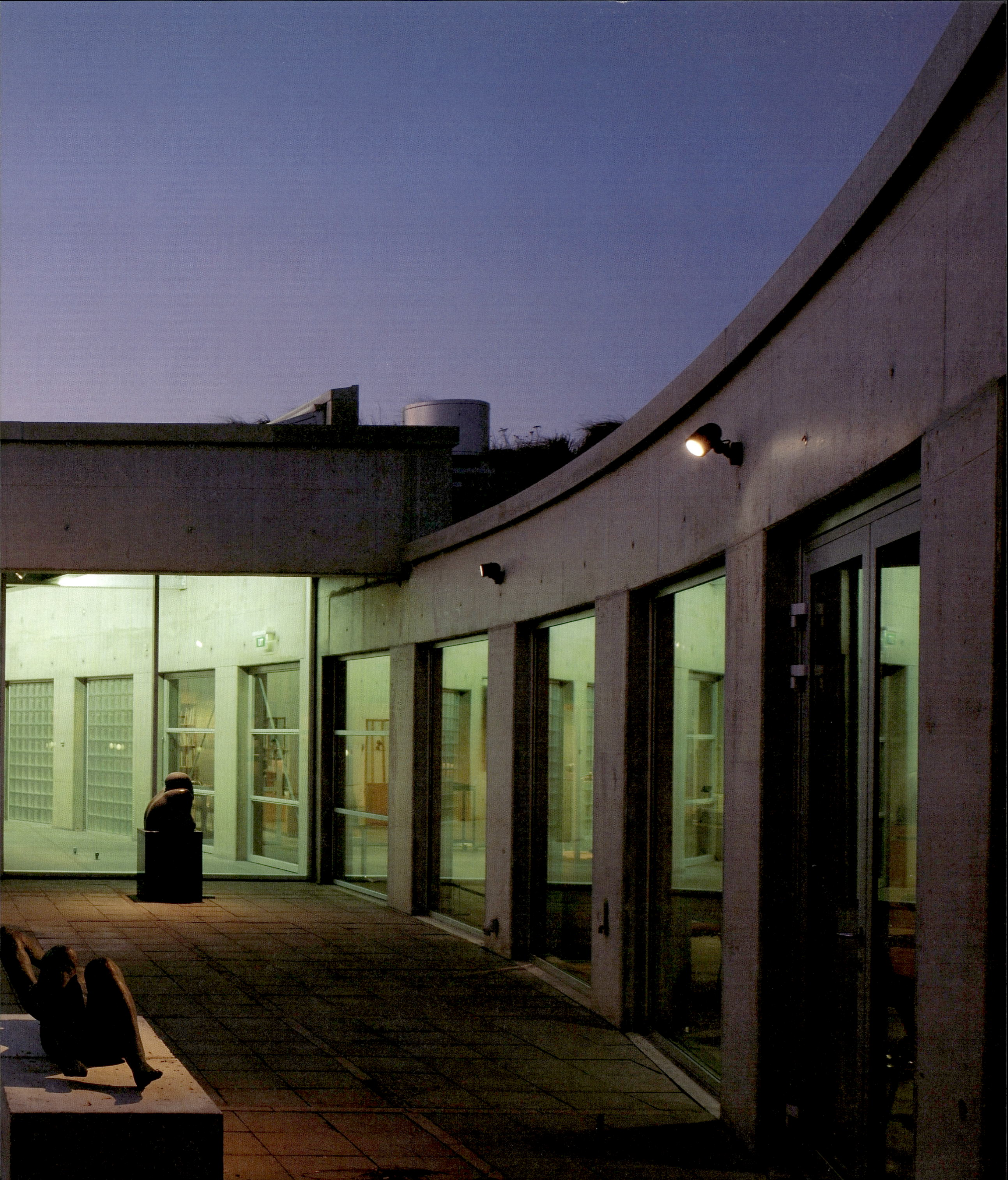

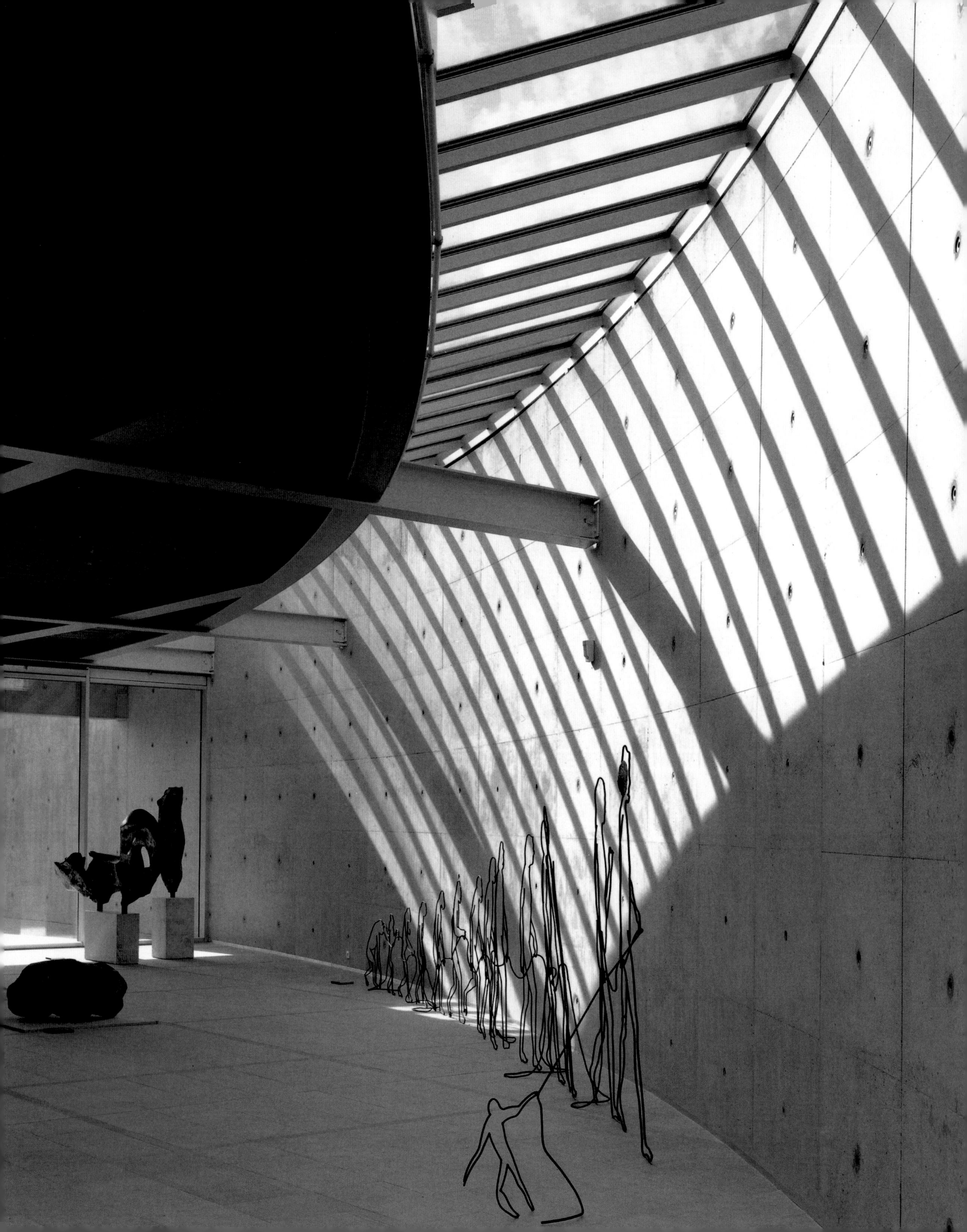

Poetry in concrete

Playing with space and time

A child with a box of bricks

This is the first time that I'm going to think about architecture. But now I've written this I begin to have my doubts. As I think about it I recall my box of bricks. I see the lid again with its colourful pictures of the buildings that could be constructed with what was to be found inside the box. I open the box once more and there we are again: the building blocks with pictures of brickwork, the slender columns, the arches, the small windows with panes of mica-glass, the triangular battlements. The things I built with them all! I remember that it was not building according to the illustrations on the lid that I enjoyed most. Best of all was thinking up something myself to build. I can still see one of my favourite buildings. After fighting hard with the laws of mechanics, which always made things wobble, slide about and collapse, I managed to make a little building which I regarded as really something. The examples on the lid were facades only behind which was nothing. But my little building had depth. Via a miniature hallway I looked into a room where light was coming through the mica windows and I remember how I would imagine that I was actually inside there, in that empty space. So now I reflect on it I must have thought about architecture some time earlier in my life, have sought for the possibility of transforming an imaginary space into a real one. My buildings were, alas, short-lived only in actual fact, for when it was time for a meal they had to be swept away from the table. My mother thought what I had made was 'lovely', but for her it was 'lovely' in the past tense only. There was a time and place for everything but now it had to be cleared away. A pity, because for a moment I had made time stand still.

The building as language

I have really no idea whether these experiences in any way correspond with the motives that make architects become architects. I know only their products, not their intentions, their wishes, the forces that drive them, conscious or not. They will have had fine, aesthetic, empathetic motives, but not so fine, opportunist, narcissistic ones too. I can guess at those from what they produce, what stands there until time tears it down again. When it comes to it, the building itself is the language in which the architect speaks to us and it is only that language that counts. A moment comes when his building is standing there, now independent of its maker. Whatever the message the maker wanted to convey with it is no longer relevant. The building's message now exists in the hearts and minds of the people who see it standing there, who walk past it, live or work in it, celebrate things in it, buy stamps or pray in it… I could go on like this forever. The only thing the architect can now 'do', is hope that what he has made is the answer to what was asked of him, the fulfilment of the wishes of his fellow creatures; in short: hope that his intentions have been understood.

I wrote that this is the first time I have been thinking about architecture and I began to have my doubts and to think that that statement was not true. And now I am beginning to have further doubts. Is what I considered untrue true, after all? I have not become an architect. In my early childhood, I did indeed feel some urge to transform imaginary spaces into real ones, imaginary time into real time. As I now realize and as is witnessed by my vivid recollections of it, it did, it is true, mean a lot to me. But it got no further than that.

I am now a visitor to the Beelden aan Zee Museum. I find myself in the position of one who wants to see sculptures. I realize I have never given architecture any thought. Of course, like anyone else, I have a whole range of cognitive and emotional reactions to the places where I happen to be. Moreover, these reactions are mainly unconscious ones. At one moment we find ourselves somewhere, but we're there, as it were, without feeling or knowing it. We look about us and see the place, but often what we are seeing does not penetrate to us and more often we don't even know that we're looking at something. We live in a recollected world, we see what we expect to see, our world has been put on a map and we know our place on that map. Nor do we realize that time is passing, that everywhere we are temporary beings. Like many others, I have experienced the world of buildings, of architecture, as a world that happened to be like that, have chosen architecture, avoided it, sought it, found it, experienced it as beautiful, ugly, interesting or boring, but nearly always without consciously asking myself about the why and wherefore of it, it just happened to be like that. And just like many others, actually I've almost always thought, no, not even thought, known, no, not even known, I have lived, I mean, with a sort of natural supposition that in the world of our buildings time stands still, that this particular world simply is. As though my relation to the world of buildings around me was not based on a continual interaction between memory and recognition, longing and fulfilment, question and answer. As though time does not move on.

Sometimes there comes a disturbance in the things we take for granted and we are confronted with the most fundamental questions concerning our existence: where am I, from where did I come, to where am I going? And that is what is happening at the moment.

Concerning the notion of loneliness

I have to reflect. And I notice that I am thinking of something I have thought about so often, but then in connection with a different subject, with poetry. What is it, after all, that moves me? In the collection of essays entitled *The Mechanics of Emotion*, I wrote: when one is moved it is as though one is reminded of something unknown to one, as though some key is opening a lock in your body and soul which you did not know you had inside you, as though you read or see something you did not realize you knew. Being moved is feeling without feeling, thinking without thought, what it contains being best approached in an attitude of: that's how it is, how it was, and how it will always be; or, in other words: this I see, not because I myself make

this of it, but because this is how it *is*. And in another collection of essays, entitled *Beautiful, but*
that's not the word for it, I hold that, actually, being moved always occurs at those moments when
we become conscious of our dual position vis-à-vis the world: the position of participant, of
our being part of the world, and that of being an outsider. Emotions have a common factor:
we realize that we belong to this world, the world gives us something of an answer to
questions about where we are, where we come from, where we are going to, and, at the
same time it becomes clear to us at that moment that the world outside 'our own world',
outside the one we are familiar with, that we remember, the 'real' world, is completely indif-
ferent to us; however much we love, hate, distrust, fear it, it goes its own way, remorselessly;
it sees us, and forgets us, at one and the same moment. It knows no time. Being moved is,
in a few words, a situation in which the unconscious naturalness of our relationship to the
world is disturbed. It is a curious, 'objective' realization, which we attempt to call grief, or
joy, but which is not that. Only the word 'loneliness' comes near to it. When we recognize the
transitoriness, the evanescence of our story about the world, we are left with this curious
loneliness.

This loneliness is conjured up by poetry. But not by poetry alone. All art does this.
Moreover, this loneliness is conjured up by everything that makes one think of the unknown.
I had not realized that buildings could do this as well. How can this be?

Loneliness and happiness

The term 'loneliness' is not usually associated with a pleasant frame of mind, still less with a
feeling of happiness. But the loneliness I mean here has everything to do with happiness.
However much happiness, too, is seen as dependent on belonging together, association with
others, our not being lonely, it is precisely the conception of loneliness that enables us to
experience the feeling of belonging together, of being linked to others. Think of our most
precious moments. We stand bent over the cradle of a new-born child. It is new, just born,
it is someone else, completely. It has come from No Man's Land, it is utterly alone, and at the
same time we are aware of our own loneliness. It is this experience that feeds our feeling of
a shared fate with this child. We know: we are alone, but we are alone together. The same
feeling can overtake us when we observe someone we love asleep in the grass. There he or
she lies, dead-still, defenceless, absent, completely alone. Then, too, we can suddenly be
aware of our own loneliness and our being linked in life to that, completely different, person.
That grassy world is not in the least interested in us. We love it, it affords us shelter, but at
the same time lets go of us. In both situations, at the side of the cradle and at the spot in the
grass, we recall the unknown, we understand that yes, life's like that, I knew it, but now I
know it again, as though I'd not realized it before: we are alone, we are transitory beings and
nothing more. I knew I was alive, but now I realize it again: I am alive, here, now, and not

 before, not afterwards, not anywhere else, no, here, now. It is a consoling loneliness difficult to put into words. One which does not separate us from others, from the world, because what we feel is: we are that, that's the way it is with us, while it is not, either, a feeling of being absorbed by the others, by the world, because we feel: I realize this, just this transitory I, I realize that with me it will disappear, leaving the others and the world behind.

Architecture: question and answer

These were a few telling examples of everyday experiences. I did not choose them to give the impression that in this museum I experience actually the same. Here there is not a soul to be seen. I chose them because the loneliness, the aloneness, I am aware of here has something vaguely to do with them, in a way which is not yet clear to me. What is 'happening' in these rooms is far removed from what happens in our everyday world, and yet, and yet, the natural things in our relations with that world are involved here too, the seamless bonds between memory and recognition, longing and fulfilment, question and answer. Yet here the questions arise which I mentioned earlier on: where am I, from where have I come, to where am I going?

How this architecture achieves this I do not know. In my poetry, I once tried to give space and time, the concrete presence of walls, roof and a ticking clock a place in the questions I mentioned, namely our loneliness and our being linked to others' lives.

New Year's Eve

It sleeps, it breathes a soft tick:
this is the house in which you live

but what is a house?

now we are together and white shadows
are dancing over our faces

now the walls and roof of this house around us
are warm and black and away

now it groans in its sleep and wakes up
and crows twelve times like a cock in the night

now our enchanted eyes shine like stars
and we separate in this selfsame house

We are inclined to think that it is the walls and roof of a house that keeps us together, that 17 the house is a shared body, and is asleep. The ticking of a clock is as natural as breathing. We don't even hear it anymore, time seems to have come to a stop. As though space and time brought us together forever. This is a misunderstanding. We ourselves create spaces, rooms, houses. We make clocks tick. Not – with their help – to belong together. On the contrary, we do this *because* we belong together. And – it seems paradoxical – this being together in a house causes the walls and roof to fall away. It is not paradoxical. It shows that it is not space which holds us together. And then, when the clock strikes as well, indicating the moment in which time simultaneously moves on and begins, we remember that being together is indissolubly linked to parting. No house can stop this from happening.

The poetic museum

My search for what lies behind my sensation of being alone in this museum has still not come to an end. Here I do not find myself in my own home with my family around me, united on New Year's Eve. But why must I think of that? On New Year's Eve one experiences something which can't be expressed in words: the simultaneous realization that space is limited and also infinite, time stands still and also marches on, as though I am looking at a frozen image from a movie. It is the motive for writing poetry: to show what can't be said, to summon up the questions about where am I, from where have I come, to where am I going? But then in such a manner that these questions are also the answers: as though the answers are precisely the awareness of those questions: there *are* no answers and that is their very essence. Poetry allows longing and fulfilment, memory and recognition to correspond for a moment.

It is really a searching for words for a poem that I am concerned with. Poetry creates a spot, a space, a moment, with words as the boundary lines, words for the walls, the roof, the clock, for instance. And if it is a good poem, these simple words together make something through which that space, that moment, becomes an emotion, a thought, or rather a realization, a speechless realization of this is how it is, it is here, this is what I am, this is what we are, united in loneliness.

This museum is like a poem. The places, the rooms, the moments it conjures up are constructed with the simple materials for walls and roof: glass, wood, steel and concrete. The structures are visible, nothing is kept concealed, nothing gives rise to questions about the construction, the building reveals its anatomy with a natural openheartedness. Simple words are used in this poetry. The sentence structure, too, is clear. Like a good poem, this language does not point to these materials and structures but to something else: to the essence of space and time. These essentials are shown with the use of simple lines, transparent transitions, open vanishing points. This building points to what is happening, not to itself, but to 'something' inside itself. It is a poetry that has nothing of the opportunist, narcissistic exhibitionism of, for example, the Groninger Museum, that strives to be something so very special in itself and thinks that you become a poem with fiery words and complicated structures. This museum seeks to be an aesthetic, empathetic workplace, a place where art acquires the space and the time to convey its existential message: we are lonely.

I look about me and I see the dead-still inhabitants of these rooms. Is a greater aloneness thinkable, palpable, conceivable? I ask myself at this moment, on seeing the aloneness of a sculpture. These bodies, stilled in a gesture, a posture, a look, these faces, eyes. It is as though space recedes, makes room, stirs them into momentary life and has them say to us, without speaking: here we are, we are coming from here, we are going to here, we are the spot, the moment, to which this building is pointing.

When I began to think about architecture, I began at the beginning: with my childhood box of bricks. I was playing. What my intentions were I can no longer recall. I wanted to make something that was not illustrated on the lid. I had a vague, imaginary picture of a room, a space, in which someone could be. I still know it had to be a solid structure and not collapse at the slightest, lightest touch. It had to be able to resist time, be permanent. I was playing with space and time. In retrospect, I think I was fantasizing about something like safety, security, permanence, and was seeking to give it outward shape. And sometimes I found that shape. Oh, what joy it gave me as I moved into that self-made space. Would the emotion that the Beelden aan Zee Museum aroused in me be an echo of that distant past? Had I since then always been playing with space and time and been looking for answers to those most elementary questions regarding loneliness and our sharing our fate?

I walk through the ever-climbing, slowly winding corridor towards the uppermost terrace. A small bronze figure of a girl stands in that infinite space. She stands quite upright, in the challenging attitude of a person who is defending herself against loneliness. She stands shining in the sun, her shadow lying at her feet. I look across the dunes, the waving grass. Once I wrote:

Go now into the garden, dear, and lie
in an empty space where the grass grows tall.
that's what I've always wanted to be,
an empty spot for someone, to stay.

Suppose that in the Dutch word for garden – 'tuin' – there was a 'd' for that 't'. Then it would be the Dutch for 'dune' – 'duin'. A difference of just one letter. That poem could have been written by the museum.

Rutger Kopland

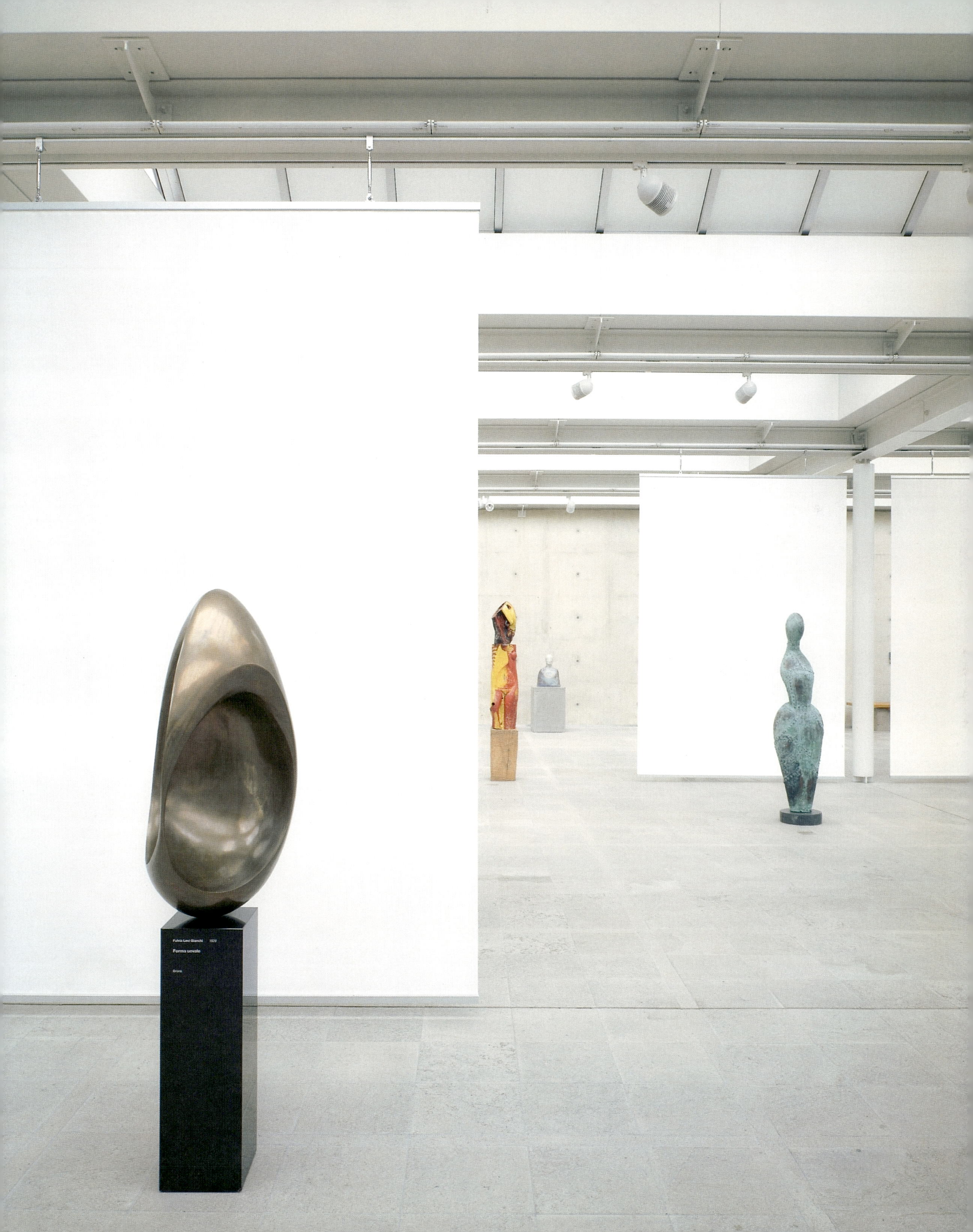
Fulvia Levi-Bianchi   1929
Forma uovale
Brons

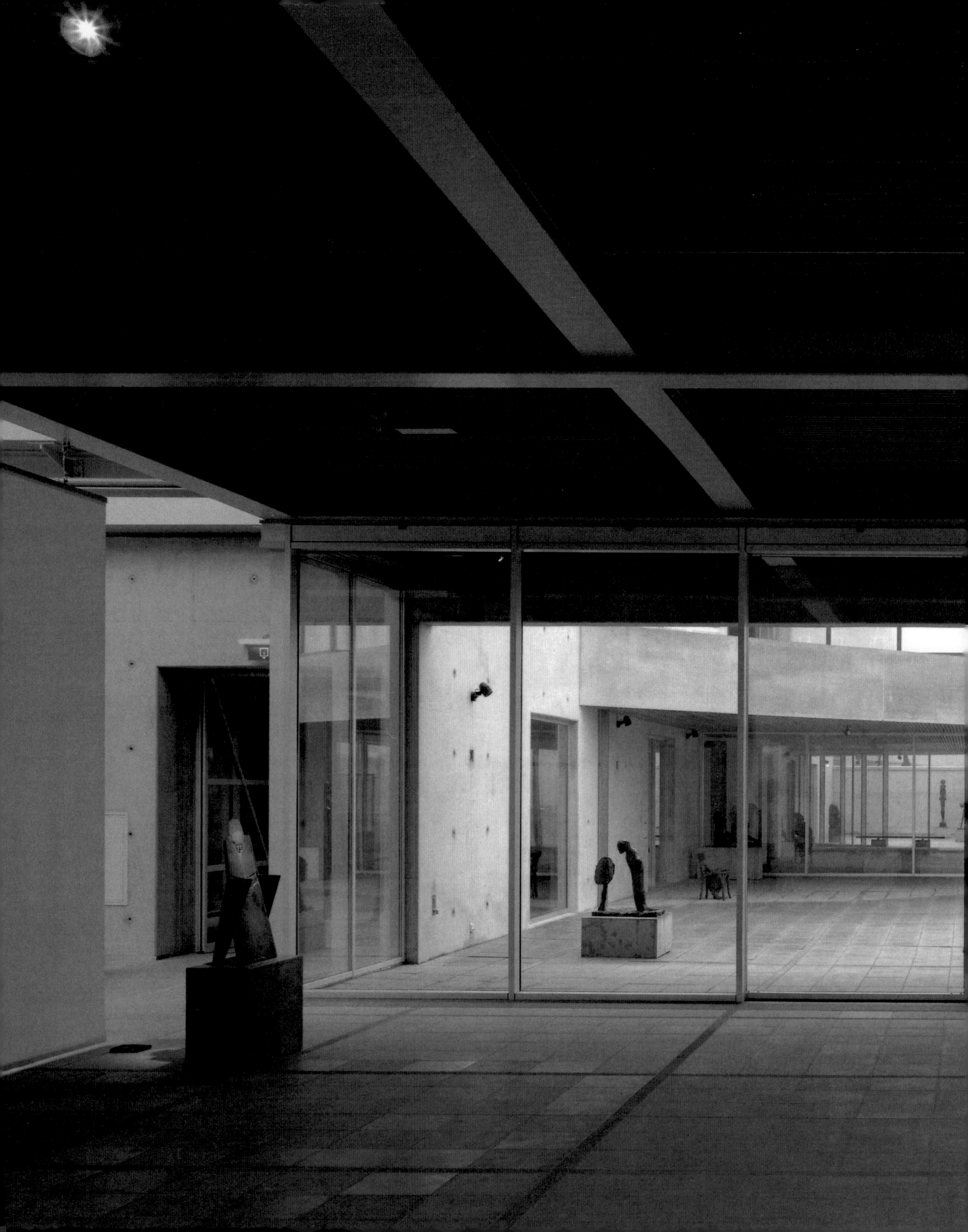

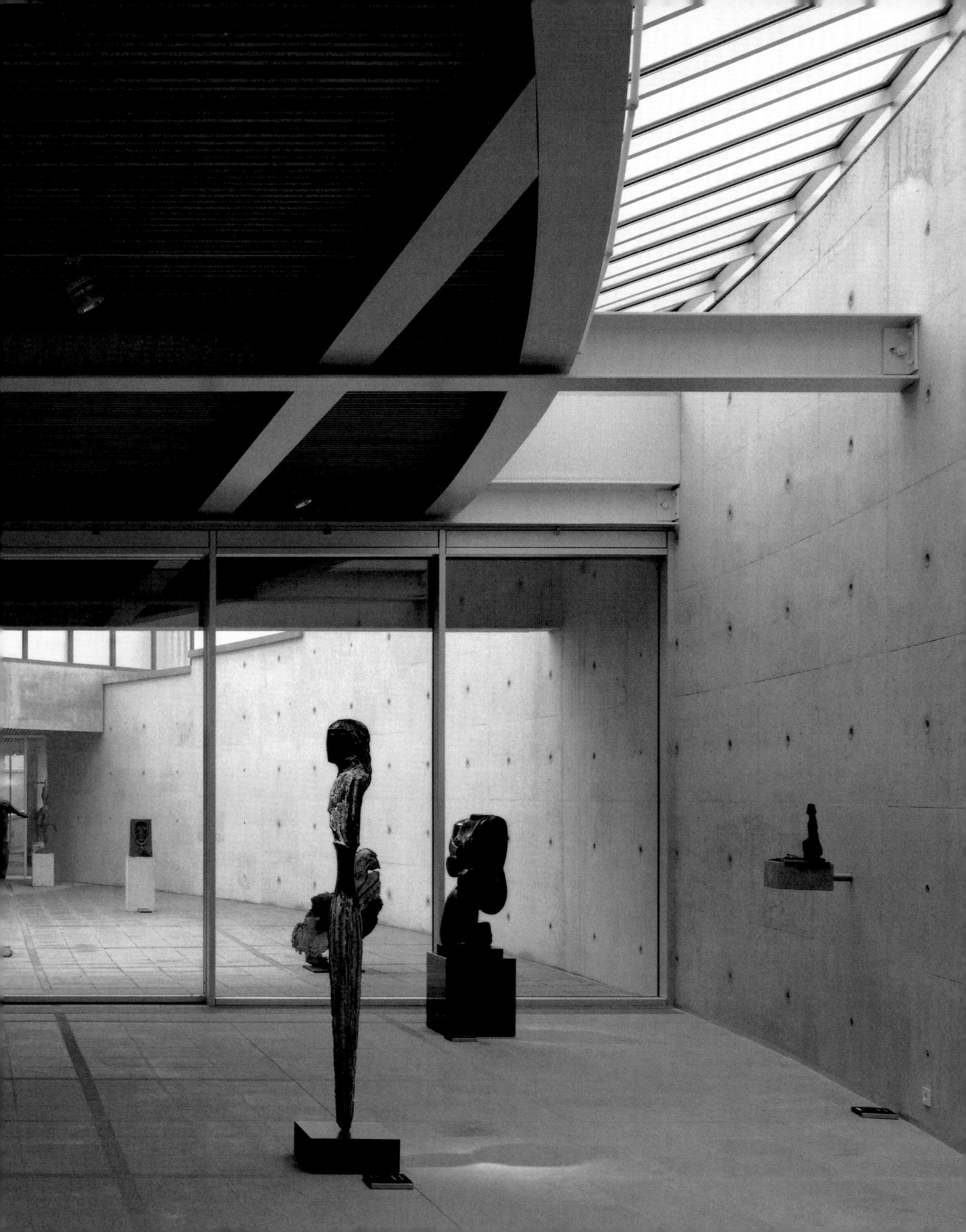

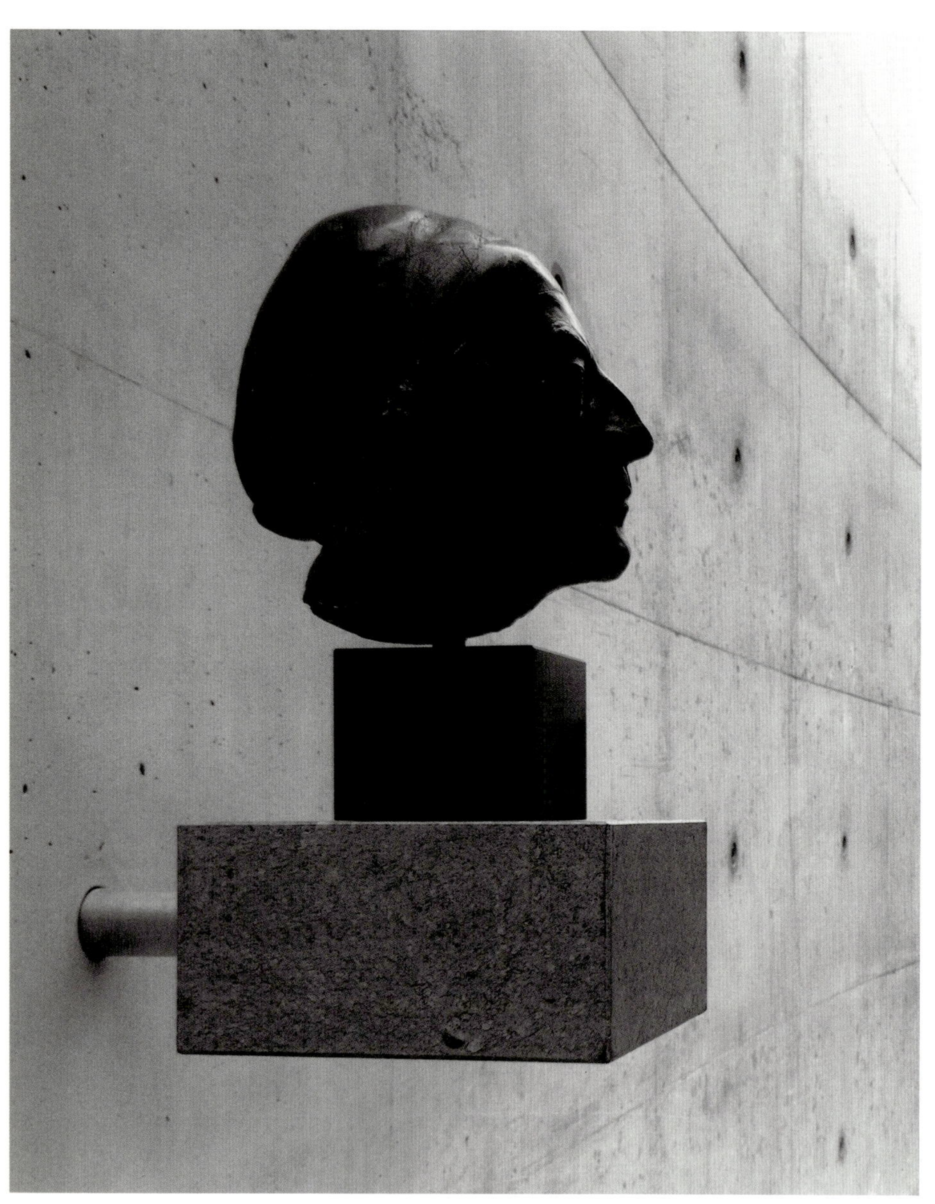

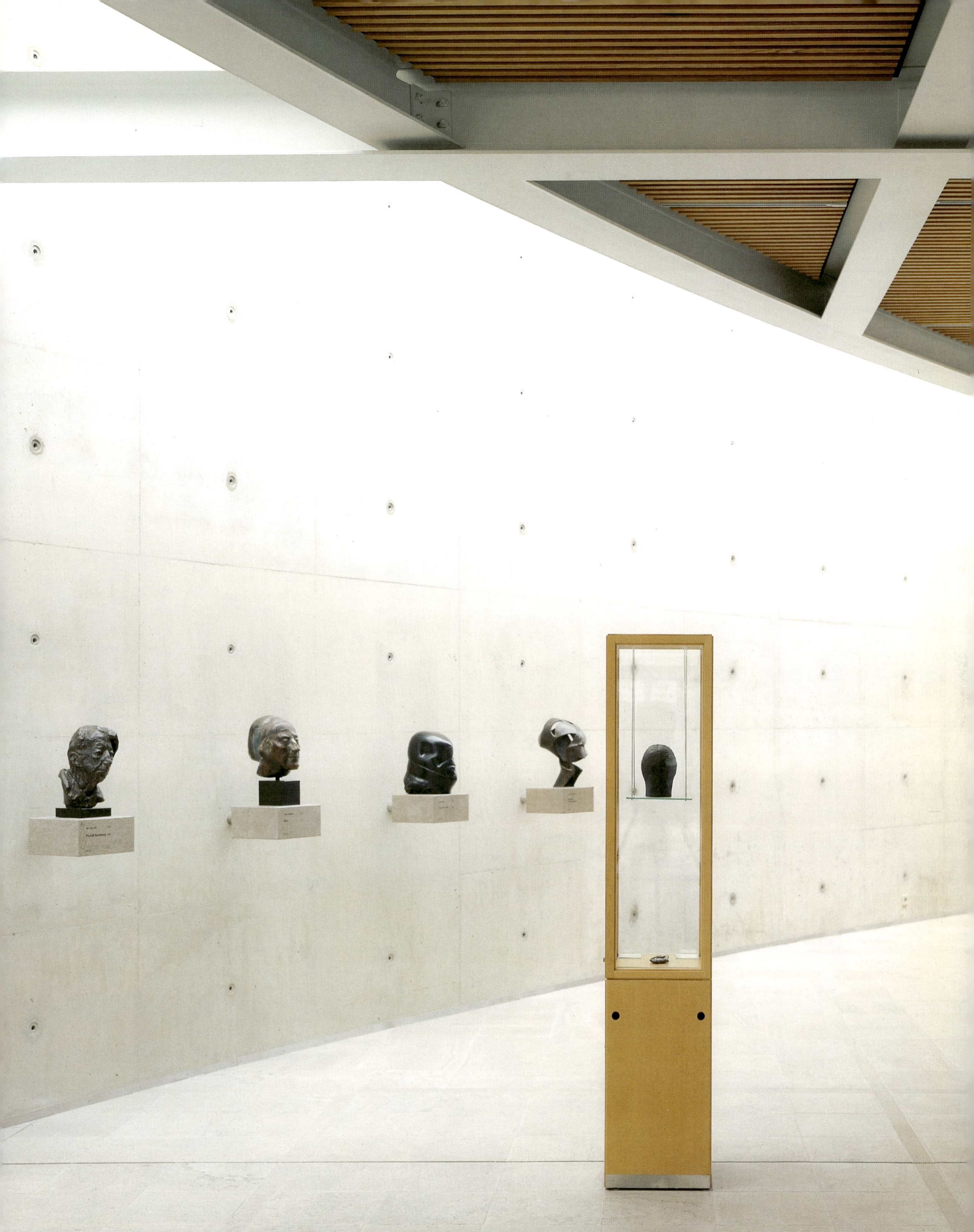

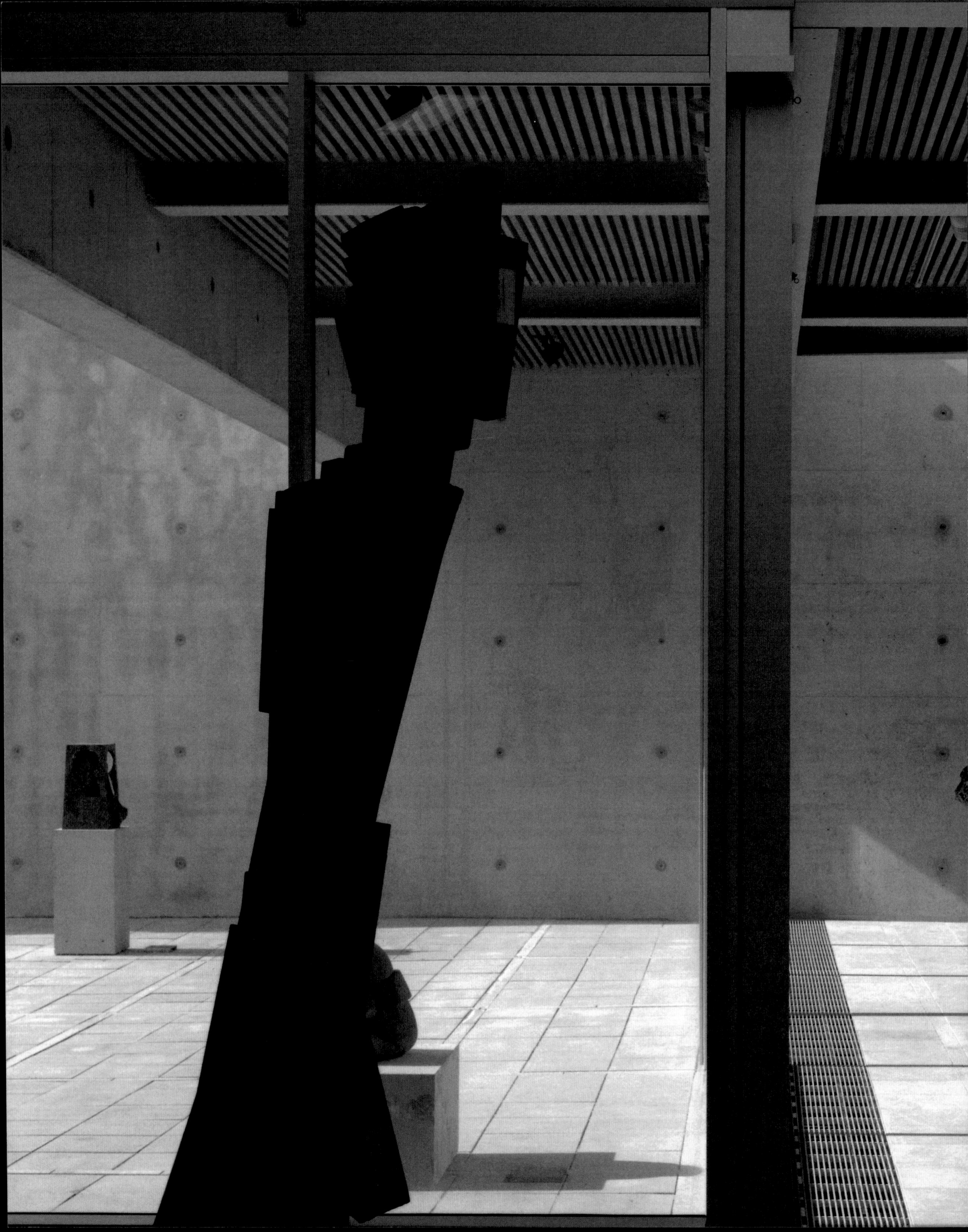

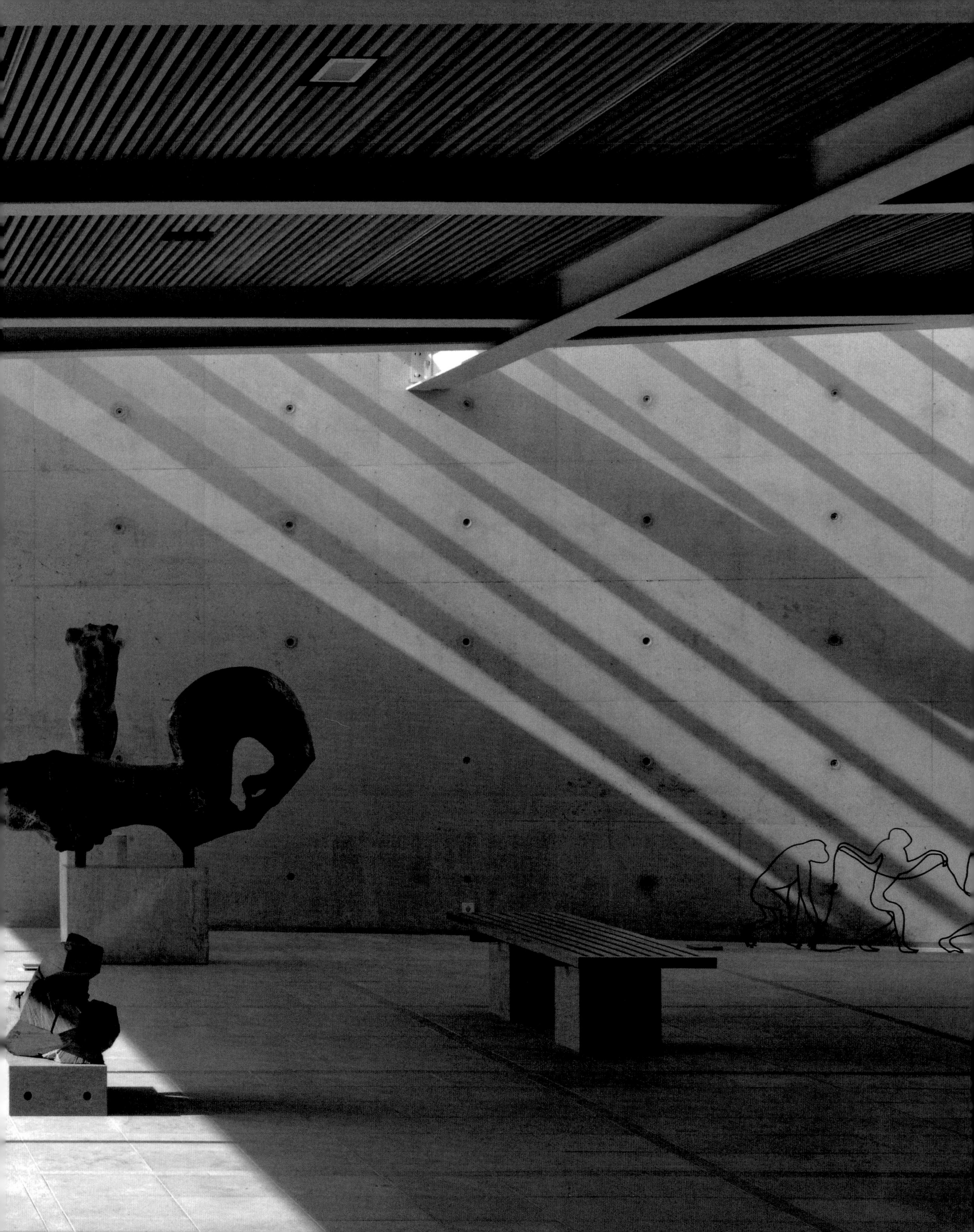

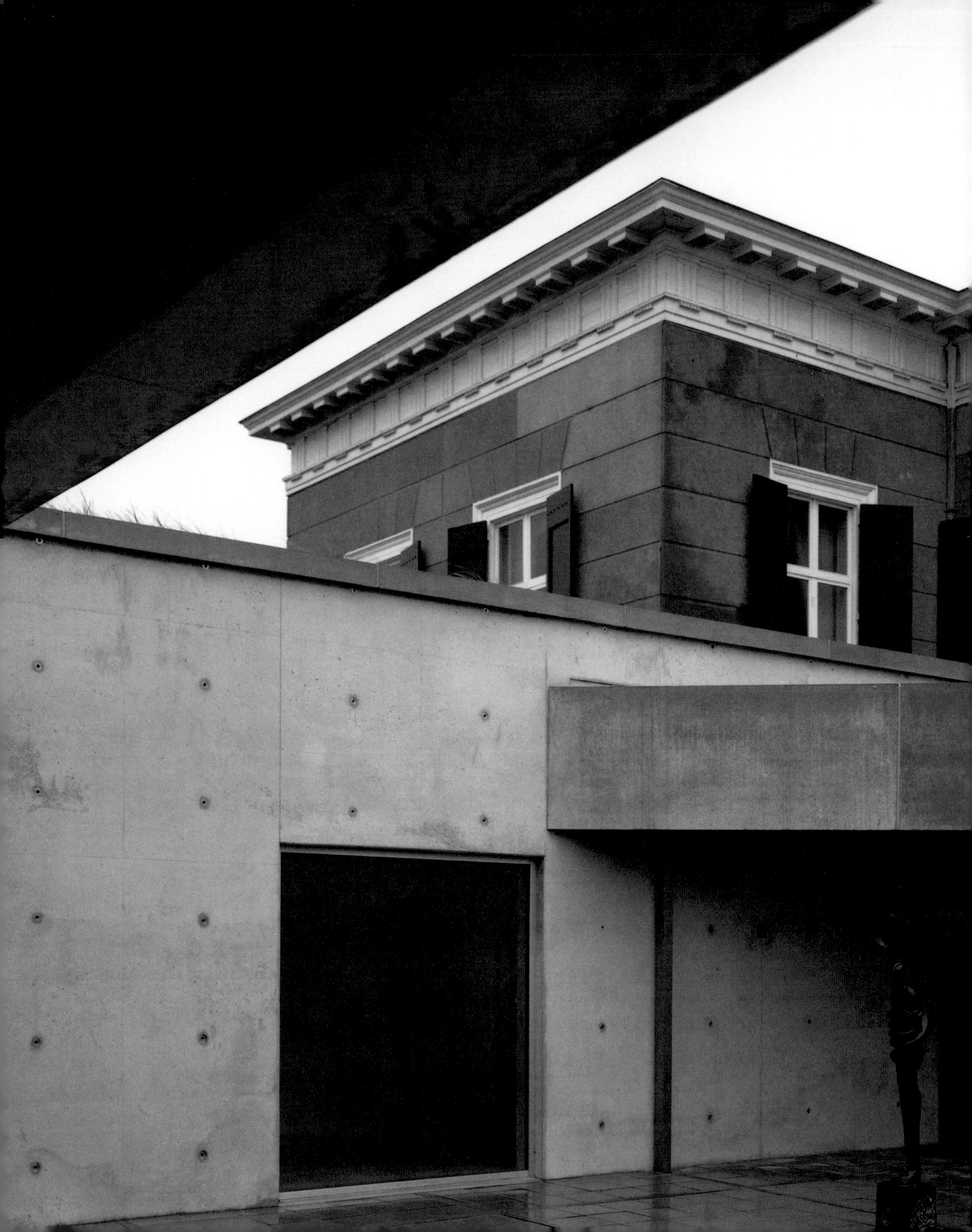

A monument on a museum pedestal

At the official inauguration of the royal Pavilion on 18 November 1827, a poem by the Scheveningen poet Cornelis Gebel[1] was presented to Queen Wilhelmina Louisa Frederica whose birthday it was and for the sake of whose health and well-being this 'wee house by the sea' had been commissioned by her husband King Willem I. This dutifully pompous occasional poem is nonetheless interesting because in its opening lines the choice of the dunes as a location for a pleasure ground is presented as something new, almost as a daring novelty; the usual choice for a quiet retreat was some charming spot with 'stately elms, the sweet song of the nightingale, fruit trees and bright flowers'.

Until the first quarter of the nineteenth century, the Dutch dune coastline was peopled chiefly by fishermen, beachcombers and villagers. As a place of residence for distinguished city folk, the dunes were too coarse, the wind too fierce and the sea too intimidating. It was not until 1825 that bathing establishments started to spring up in Zandvoort and Scheveningen, for it was only then that the seashore became a fashionable destination for citizens of the young Dutch nation. Ideas about the healthy sea air, the unspoilt wild dune landscape, the dazzling light above the foaming waves on the shoreline, date from this time. The cities were impoverished, unhygienic and unhealthy; small wonder that those who could afford it went in search of fresh air.

As such, the royal Pavilion is a superlative 'cultural-historical monument, a manifestation of the culture of sea bathing in the days when this culture, following the English example, was starting to take hold in the Netherlands in the early nineteenth century. ... As one of the last relics of that culture, the Von Wied Pavilion occupies a special place in this seaside resort architecture. The open situation on top of a dune with a direct relationship to the sea recalls the characteristic aspects of this culture.'[2]

28   Nor was the chosen site on the Scheveningen shore without historical significance, for it would have reminded Willem and Wilhelmina of their landing on that same shore on 30 November 1813.

The aforementioned occasional poet called the Pavilion 'a proud edifice that will endure for centuries, [that will] withstand the hurricane on steadfast walls… a magnificent pleasure palace'. The building, designed by Adriaan Noordendorp, Bouwmeester der Koninklijke Paleizen en Landsgebouwen (Royal Architect), is perfectly in keeping with the spirit of the time: neo-classical, romantically placed in the landscape and picturesquely detailed. The interior is embellished with stucco references to the sea: sea horses, tridents, shells, corals and starfish.

The Pavilion did not remain in splendid isolation for long. No sooner had it been completed than it was joined by the Badhuis (public bathing-house) and a public access road, the Badhuisweg, on which the Hotel Galerie was established and along which the well-to-do soon started to erect seaside villas. The best impression of what was then a very exclusive seaside resort is to be found in the Mesdag Panorama, which the artist and five fellow-painters completed in 1881. While the Pavilion is not entirely alone, it still dominates the horizon as a detached post, a monument standing high atop the dune.

Nothing is so changeable as a monument

While the changes to the building itself were negligible, its surroundings underwent a huge transformation during the first seventy-five years. On all sides of the generous four-hectare plot, buildings were built and rebuilt, roads laid and relocated. Thus seaside tourism took its toll around the Pavilion.

After the death in 1919 of Willem's granddaughter, Princess Marie, who was married to Willem von Wied, the Pavilion changed hands twice before it was eventually sold to the Vereeniging van de Nieuwe of Littéraire

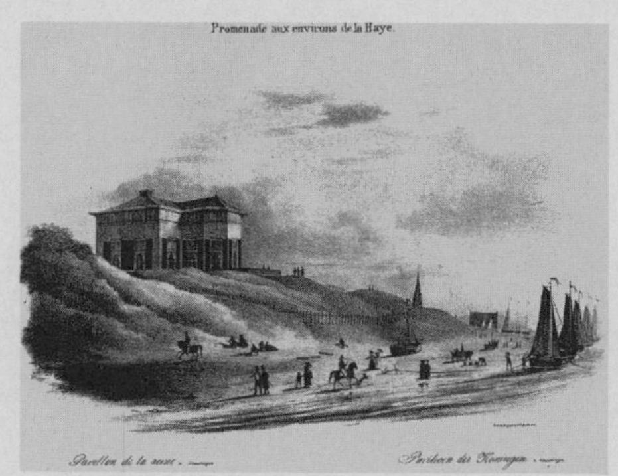

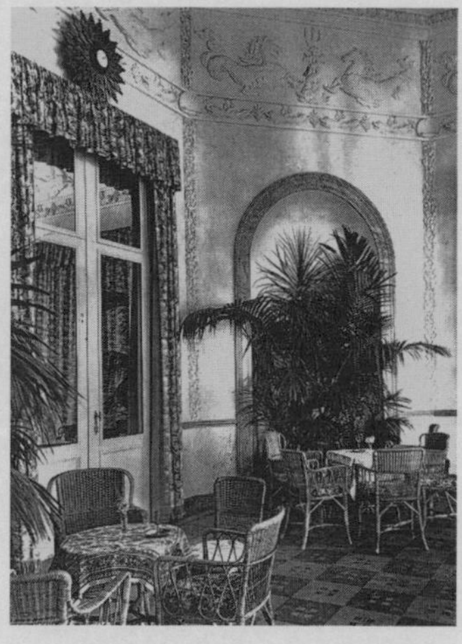

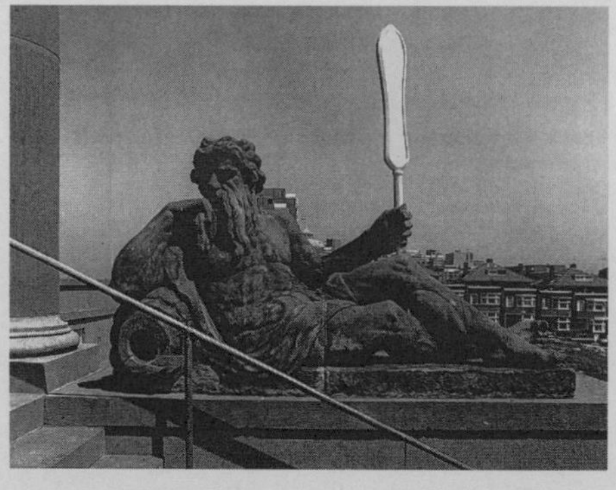

Sociëteit De Witte (a Hague literary society established in 1918) as an out-of-town annex and summer pavilion for the members. The terraces were altered and the surrounding land was sold off and developed. During the Second World War, the Pavilion was inside the German *Sperrgebiet* (restricted area) where the occupying forces wreaked havoc.

Windows, doors and ceilings were badly damaged by the explosions. After the war, it was the turn of precious youth to despoil this inviting building. On the landward side, the huge recumbent stone river gods guarding the entrance had their arms and legs knocked off. In 1946, in an effort to prevent further deterioration, the architect S. de Clerq was put in charge of a restoration scheme which went no further than the repair of wartime damage. By 1956 radical restoration was needed. The drawing up of the restoration plan and the supervision of its execution were entrusted to the Hague architect Jan Wils. In 1978 and again in 1994, further restoration work was necessary. Ravaged by the salt sea wind, acid rain, damp and frost, the Pavilion requires continuous maintenance and renewal of materials.

Viewed long term, it appears that though a universally admired monument may be preserved by material efforts, it may equally well be afflicted by loss of function, fashionable interventions and vicissitudes when regard for the monument or for its surroundings wanes.

The building history of the Pavilion shows that the preservation of this object has been arduous but ultimately successful; that the direct relationship to the sea has never been broken, but that incessant interventions in the surroundings have all but nullified its value as a 'seaside retreat'.

It is interesting to note that in the course of its 170-year existence, this monumental building has acquired a completely different environment, a different purpose, a different occupant, a different name and finally — figuratively, but to some extent also literally — a different foundation. The tendency of each generation to adapt what it inherits to its own times is irresistible. Even monuments do not escape this fate. A firm anchorage in the fast-flowing current of time increases the chances of survival.

The Pavilion had lost its meaning as a seaside retreat. Its remaining function, as a society annex during the summer months, was too marginal to justify the considerable and recurrent cost of restoration and maintenance. The building had no clear function and this threatened its cultural-historical significance. The building history of a monument adds the argument of 'purpose' to our evaluation of it. For a monument, meaningful survival implies a strategic adjustment to each successive period of its history. Just how reasonable do professionals and the general public find this argument about a change of purpose to suit the times? This is the crucial question facing those charged with the preservation of historic monuments, one they must attempt to decide impartially in each instance.

A new foundation is required

A sculpture museum, an initiative of the Stichting De Onvoltooide set up by Mr and Mrs Scholten, would give new meaning to the Pavilion. Beneath the Pavilion's Zeezaal and on either side of the building, within and below the dune, Wim Quist designed with great sensitivity a more or less subterranean museum with a view of the sea and the Dutch skies. A lack of space at ground level was solved by an intensification of the site. The Crown had already declared in a Royal Decree of 11 June 1987 that 'development [can] only be acceptable here if, by dint of careful design, strictly limited height and a discreetly visible volume, it fits in with the Pavilion in such a way that this monument continues to dominate its surroundings.' To the extent, of course, that the densely built surroundings did not already dominate the monument!

On the seaward side, at any rate, the Pavilion continues to determine the appearance of the dune, displaying itself on a new pedestal: the Beelden aan Zee Museum.

Meticulous design became the hallmark of this commission and it has been uniquely realized by Wim Quist. To begin with there was the delineation of the museum location and the natural relationship with the dune. Seen from the vantage point of the boulevard, the sand-coloured concrete walls curve protectively to left and right of the Pavilion along the flanks of the dune, like two outstretched wings come to rest. Equally symmetrical is the gently sloping enclosure of the retaining walls on Pellenaerstraat. The articulation of the concrete elements is achieved by finely indented edge profiles reminiscent of the horizontal detailing of the Pavilion.

The deepening and layout of the old Pavilion cellars is particularly inventive. The vaults span sober archways, creating the impression of a Romanesque space that is eminently suitable for a striking display of sculptures. The material usage is crisp; the spatial line is fluid and echoes the natural incline of the dune.

The symmetrical terraces of the Pavilion return as a formal rhyme in the symmetry of the museum terraces. These references from new to old make it clear that the historic monument was one of the sources of inspiration for Quist's architecture. Although they are not in the least historicizing, the skylights above the indoor section of the museum play with the form of the tympanum which thus becomes a kind of symbol for the entire situation.

The symmetrical layout of the museum parallels the classical symmetry of the Pavilion. Another parallel is the interpretation of their respective functions. From its terraces and windows, the Pavilion offers a prospect of the sea. Beelden aan Zee offers a panorama of the 'human image' because this was the theme the collectors took as their starting point. The panorama offered by Beelden aan Zee will change with each successive generation because the interpretation of the human image is different for every generation.

What will remain unchanged on this spot, is the marvellous surprise of the shifting view of the sea, of the shifting play of light on the plasticity of the monument *and* on the plasticity of the sculptures by the sea.

Fons Asselbergs

1
Quoted in: 'Een koninklijk paviljoen en een museum aan zee', *VOM-reeks* 1994, no. 2, The Hague.
2
Recommendation of the National Historic Monuments Commission, 24.3.1993.

A casemate for art

I vividly recall my visit to the Beelden aan Zee Museum when Charlotte van Pallandt was exhibiting there. Seldom have exhibition and museum complemented one another so perfectly, indeed, enhanced one another.

First the artist: she saw abstract art come and (almost) go. She outlived the age of black squares, ready-mades, monochromes and pop art. What Ortega y Gasset has called the 'dehumanization of art', she casually ignored. A whole age of misanthropy made scarcely any impact on her. She continued making sculptures of people as sculptures have always been made of people. Hatred of the human body never oppressed her spirits. She was born before the publication of Freud's *The Interpretation of Dreams*. Human beings were still in full possession of their mental faculties. The idea that there could be an inner being that lay outside our control was a theoretical impossibility. A hundred years on, we are delighted if we discover that there is at least *something* that is still within our control. Humanity was ousted from the centre of things. But it mattered not to her. Decade after decade she went on producing portraits, sculptures, of self-possessed human beings, figural studies in which the beauty of the human body was never in doubt. Brancusi, Zadkine, Perlmuter – they would have meant little to her. Perhaps she did not even notice the passage of the last hundred years.

Charlotte van Pallandt – she just missed completing her first century – was perfectly at home in the new Beelden aan Zee Museum in Scheveningen. Her work testifies to an unswerving belief in human figuration. Even the sculptures she made in the 1980s, with their rough and irregular surface, have more to do with old age as an inextricable part of a full life, than with deformity and despondency. I must confess that I do not understand how an artist could have managed to remain more or less aloof from every avant-garde movement. History is certainly present in her works, but not as subject. At most in a number of stylistic elements that Van Pallandt adopted from others. In terms of content, the work is timeless.

This is also precisely the selection criterion for the Scholten-Miltenburg collection on show in the museum. It is not only the founders who have remained unreservedly faithful to the principle of eternity, but also the artists whose works they have acquired over the years. Not a single work is about 'the end of humanity'. On the contrary, there is scarcely a trace of doubt to be seen. They include some truly wonderful sculptures although I must admit that I do not really understand them in the context of their time.

And then the building where this is to be seen. A new museum by Wim Quist, whose extension of the Kröller-Müller Museum is regarded by many as a benchmark in museum design. A more fitting building for this collection is unimaginable. Seldom has architecture been so abstract and at the same time such a perfect expression of its function. In the midst of that model of urban incompetence called Scheveningen, stands an archaic apparition, a subterranean sanctuary for higher spheres. Composed of elementary geometrical shapes, constructed of good, honest concrete, the museum is an agreeable anomaly amongst all the brash commercial activity. This building is undeniably intended as a pure note amidst the tumult of beach volleyball.

The highlight of the tour of the museum is the centrally located Sea Room. The view of the surfboard-infested foreground is blotted out by the edge of the dune. Only unsullied vistas meet the gaze. An immaculate, empty ocean under a continually changing firmament. And suddenly it comes to me. The reason why this museum is so superlatively apposite is that it invokes precisely the atmosphere that is required for its function. It is a bunker, a casemate for art. The outlook is not for the purpose of future conquest, but to facilitate vigilance. The human image, the body, the precious jewel of creation, is being guarded here in Quist's Atlantic Wall. O, how I detest the irony of this point.

Ole Bouman

A museum that welcomes

Granted, it was not easy to produce a reasonably balanced reaction to a visit (in my case visits) to Beelden aan Zee. I was hampered mainly by a bit of professional myopia which, though rooted in the past, is still the first filter through which I gaze on such occasions: I cannot help looking first and longest at the building. The word 'building' is out of place here for a start, for what the master-architect has accomplished here with his client completely eludes our standard lexicon.

Something quite different has occurred here. The gigantic bronze mask by Mitoraj, that seems lost on the seaward side of the dune, is missing an ear. To find it you must follow the panels of the concrete retaining wall. Quist dug this ear out of the dune and there, in the middle of the auricle, he discovered the Von Wied pearl which has been allowed to remain where it was. I used to reflect quite a lot on 'organic' architecture and I was even able to realize one or two examples of the genre. Only a few clients proved to be ripe for it. But now, perhaps jolted awake by the orgy of postmodernism, various bits and pieces of organic 'material' have suddenly started turning up in recent decades. By no means all of it is well-founded, and none of it can stand in the little bit of shadow cast by Beelden aan Zee. Here the building has been quite literally 'discovered' and freed from the dune with archeological circumspection. What is more, it has also stabilized this heap of shifting sand in the technical sense, such that one can only gaze with astonishment and admiration at the extremely subtle, but always simple detailing of in themselves gigantic building parts.

The total absence of portentous monumentality in this museum ranks it among a handful of museums in the world that have no need of the temple front, the towers, the jettied storeys, the rigid symmetry, the eclectic toying with all manner of building styles in order to guard and display their valuables. The initial encounter with Beelden aan Zee is rather halting. This 'organism' does not give itself immediately. It does not strive to impress and neither does it thrust itself upon you; it does not shout from afar: here I am! It does not flaunt itself and neither does it oppress; it welcomes.

Once inside there is a sense of relief, calm, of coolness and warmth at the same time and – without becoming cosy – intimacy. The layout, without immediately disclosing all its secrets, is clear in that it suggests a natural routing. The indoor and outdoor spaces may be bounded by regular walls, but they are unusually shaped, irregular spaces. They withdraw self-effacingly vis-à-vis the exhibited work. In the centre of the plan two stunning surprises await. The Von Wied pearl turns out to possess (or to have been given?) an extremely interesting foundation. It is quite enough to awaken religious feelings, though its dimensions are free of monumentality. At one time there was a wonderful, religiously inspired sculpture in the 'apse', but I have sorely missed it on my latest visits. As you leave the 'church' again, the image of the sea so dear to the Dutch unfolds before your eyes. That this image should also evoke the association of a bunker, is pretty well inevitable since *The Longest Day*, but here, apart from one or two less appealing boulevard artefacts, it is one of immense serenity. It must be the framing by the dune with its undulating planting of marram grass that renders it so peaceable and restful.

Then the splendid, gradually ascending terraces come into view with – in contrast to the skylight illumination of the main room – direct daylight (light *and* wind!). The two small outdoor patios (north and south) provide space for intimate exhibitions. The south patio now seems to be permanently devoted to the portraits of the royal family. Indeed, it would be difficult to imagine a more appropriate place in the museum for Arthur Spronken's *chef d'oeuvre*. And finally there is the large patio that is physically con-

nected with the main room and the museum café and is usually visited on the way back.

The dominant impression, in form, material and above all in colour, is of a building intent on withdrawal. The interior automatically assumes the colour of the light so that indoors remains in touch with outdoors. Which to my mind brings us to the *raison d'être* of Beelden aan Zee: the sculptures. You can argue and disagree about the strength and effectiveness with which the individual pieces of sculpture convey the human image to the viewer; any differences either way cannot at any rate be blamed on the ambience. Besides, the museum's own collection provides such a diversity of human images that individual opinions cannot but differ. But that is in the nature of human beings surely? Doesn't the human image throw up a host of images that are (and remain) light years away from one another? Images that are capable of filling us by turns with the greatest tenderness, the deepest emotion but equally, too, with loathing and revulsion. From Wenckebach, Meefout and Gallo, via Sato, Begbie, Spronken to... Bühl perhaps. I encountered very little of the negative side of the scale in the permanent collection. That may not always be the case in temporary exhibitions. Yet who am I but a 'carpenter' who can but pass a very modest judgement on such matters.

In short, since 1994, the human image as depicted in contemporary sculpture has a home by the sea that appeals in an exceptionally powerful fashion to the total imagination.

Joost van der Grinten

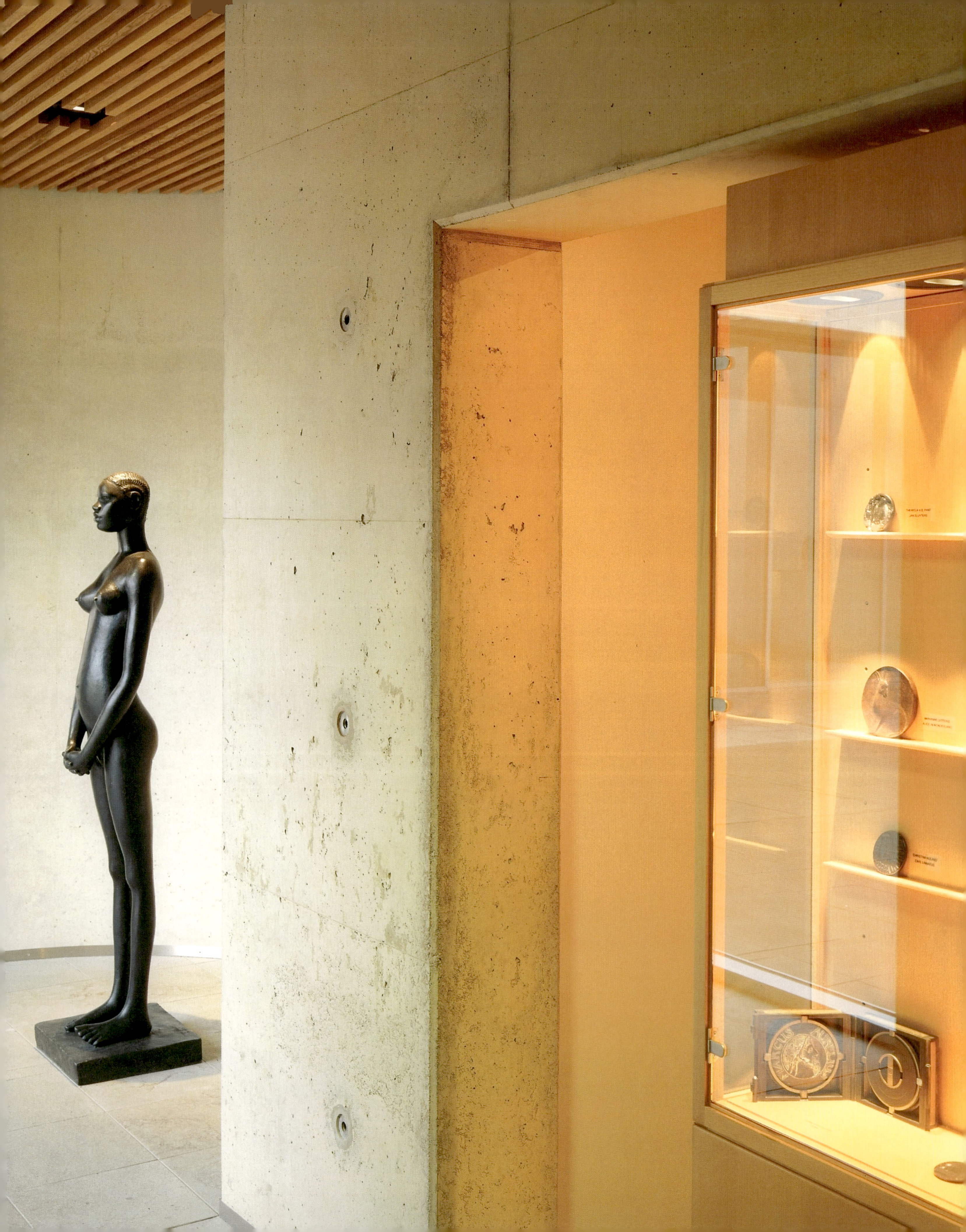

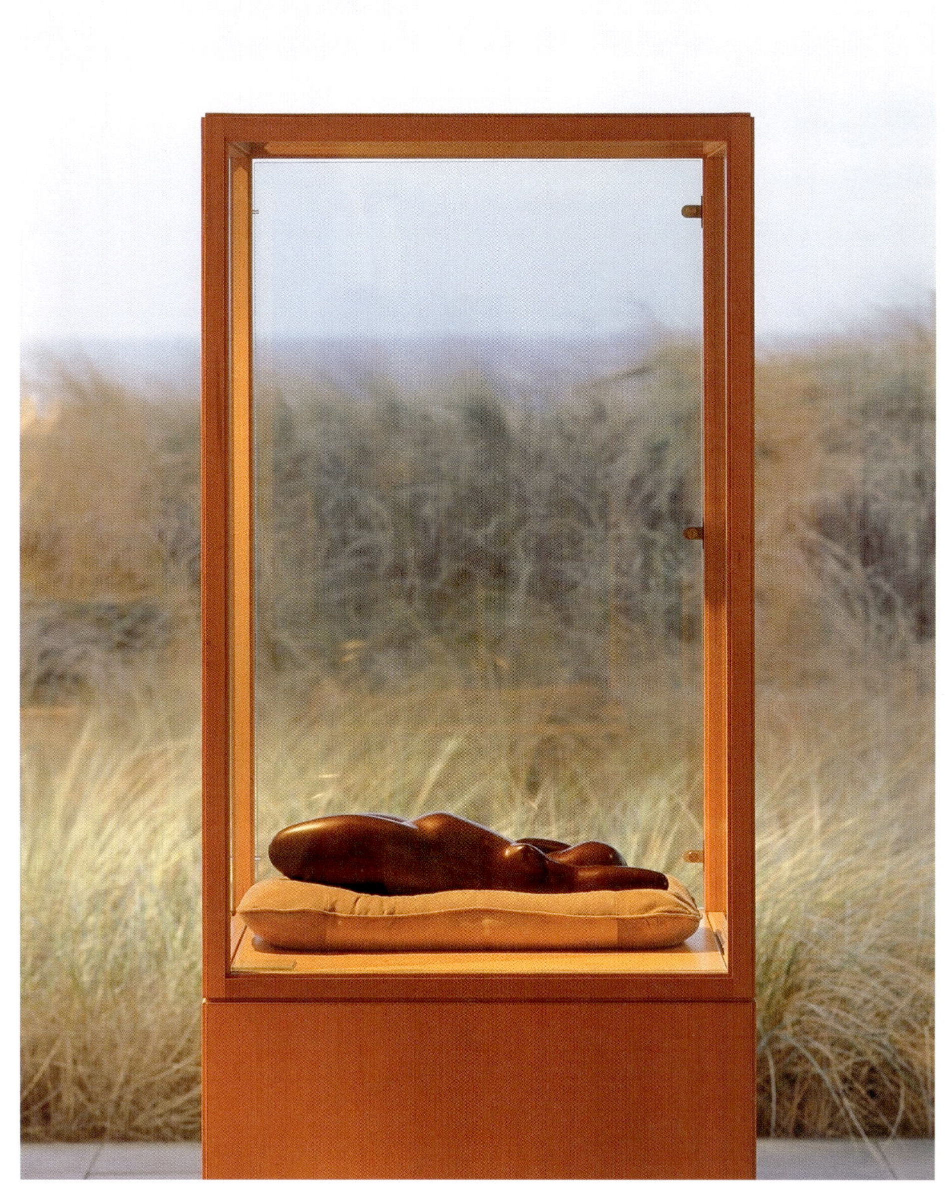

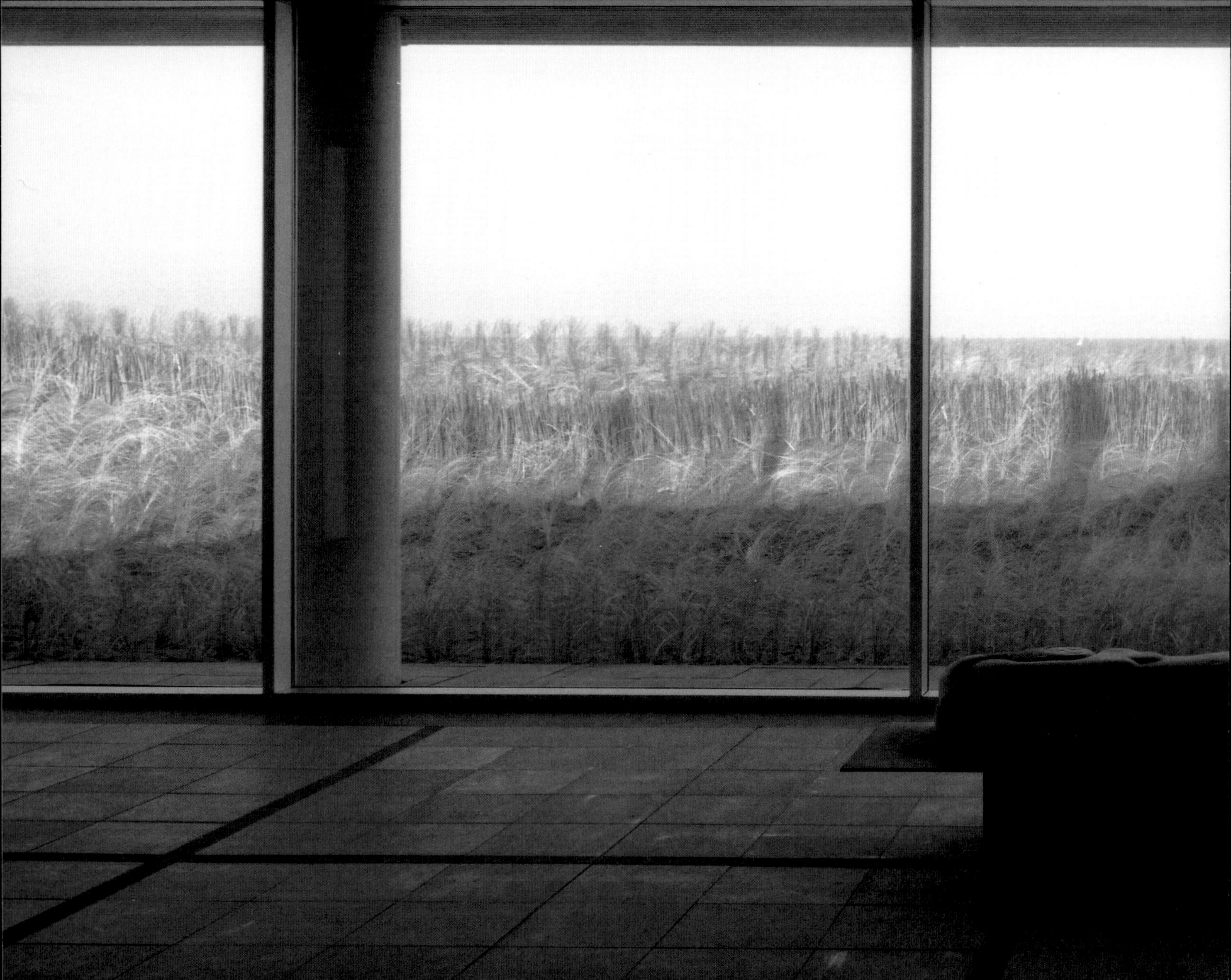

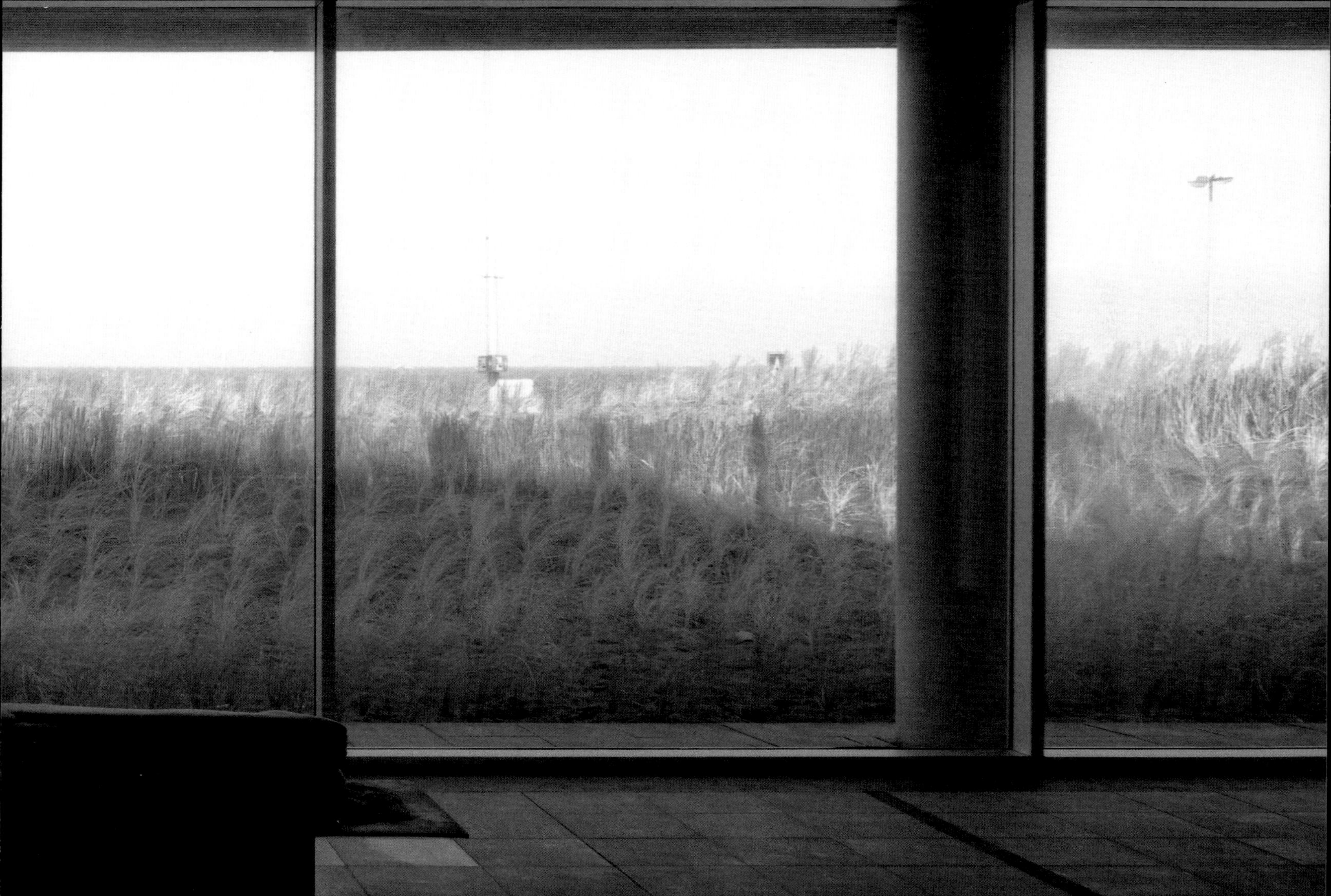

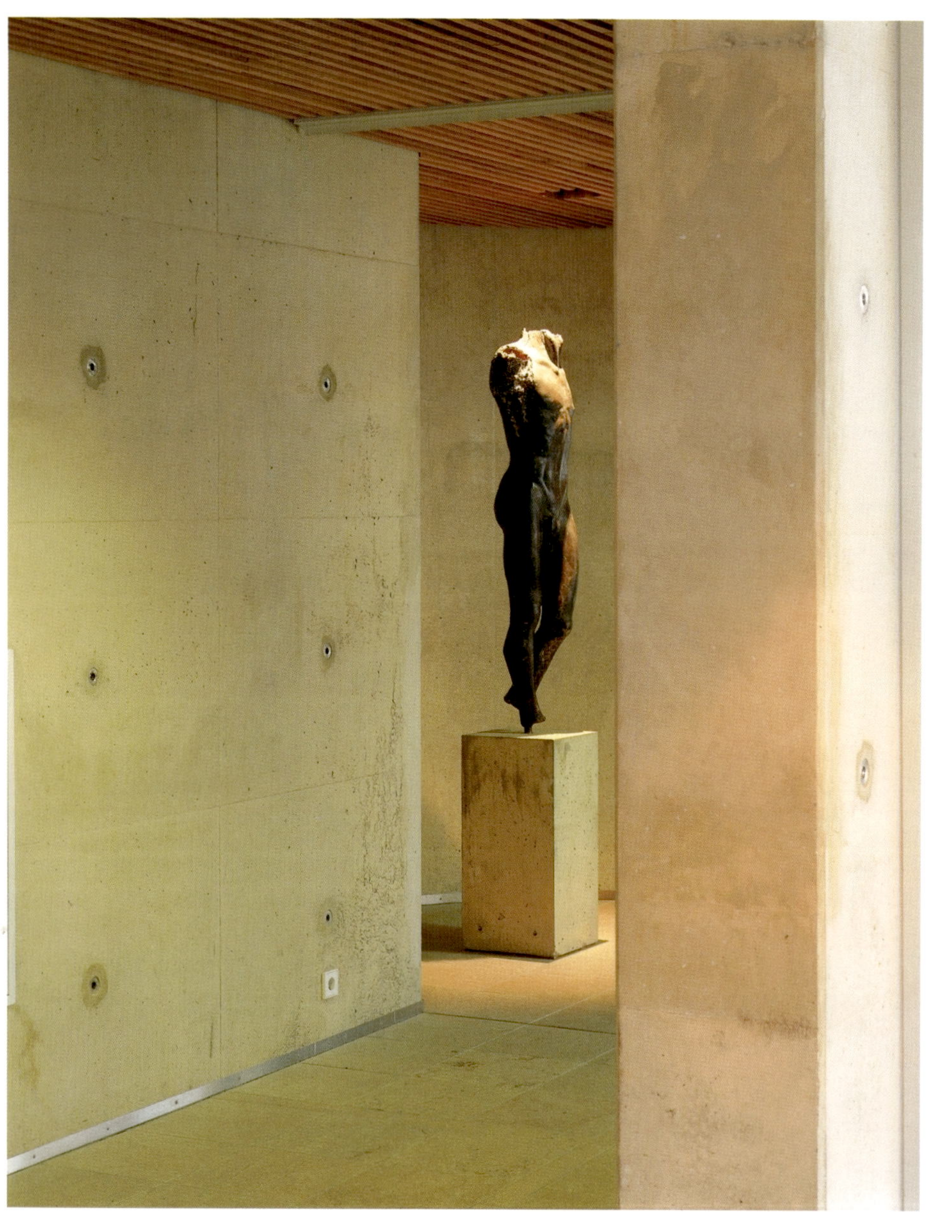

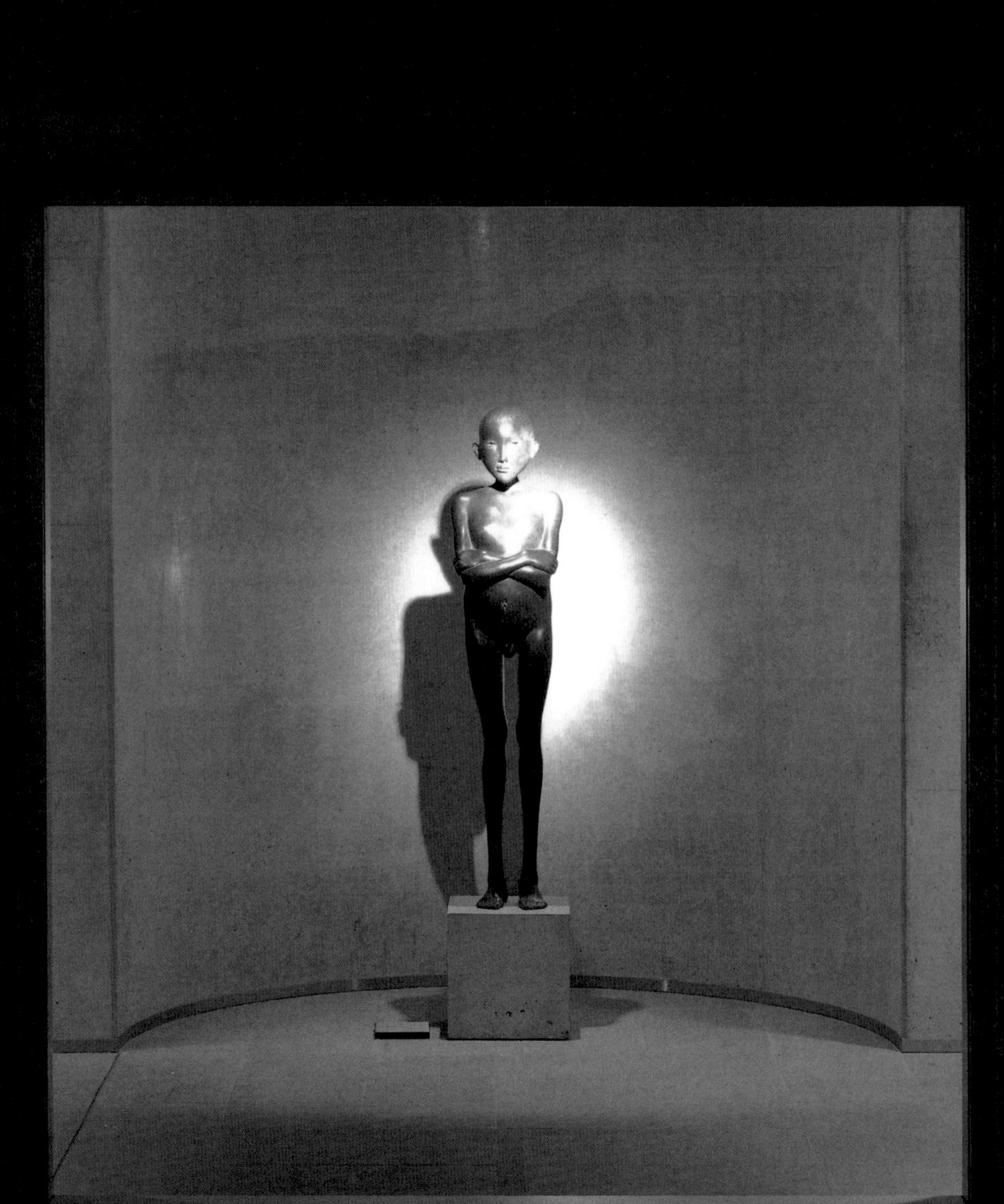

Architect and client

People who know about these things say that the relation between architect and client affects the outcome of the commission. At first glance, this does not sound implausible. Indeed, the reverse seems rather unlikely. It is inconceivable that people who, in a situation of mutual dependency, are closely involved in a creative process, should not exert a certain influence on the end product. So it does not seem out of place in a discussion of that result – the Beelden aan Zee Museum – to describe that relationship. Granted, the two parties may felt differently about this relationship, but given the purpose of the book in which this essay appears, it is logical that only the client's version should be heard here. The important question whether the outcome of that collaboration has, architecturally speaking, been positive or negative, is not one I shall be addressing. It is not easy for the client to pass judgement on this; nor, for that matter, for the architect, although he will usually be able to reach some kind of assessment on the basis of comparison. Be that as it may: this is for others to pronounce on, if necessary.

Why does the client choose a particular architect? This question presupposes another one, namely: why a new building? To fully appreciate the answer to this, one first needs to know something about the client and the object of the commission.

The client and the object of the commission

The initiative for the construction of the Beelden aan Zee Museum was taken by my wife and myself. It is a genuine 'joint' venture. This applies to the idea of a museum and it also applies to the choice of architect for the museum building. My wife and I conducted the groundwork, in the sense of visiting dozens of museums around the world, together. We also conducted virtually all the discussions with the architect during the design phase together. This elucidation is important because I am the one who is writing this essay (the content of which also has my wife's approval, incidentally) and because architecture is more my hobby than hers. This hobby of mine was not always an advantage as it turned out. I shall come back to this later.

Originally, we had no idea of building a special museum for our collection. On the contrary. For a long time we were firmly of the opinion that we did not want our own museum. That this is nonetheless what eventually happened has several causes, of which I shall mention two important ones.

In the first place, it gradually became clear to us that it is very difficult, if not impossible, to find a satisfactory home base for a specific collection such as ours. In the context of this essay, I shall say no more on this point. The second cause also has to do with experience. The idea of a museum for our collection arose when we were living in Bilthoven, in a spacious house set in a large garden. When the idea of our own museum did eventually arise, we never considered realizing it on the basis of the existing house. Why not? For the simple reason that we had seen it done in various places in the world – in Denmark and England among others – and in each instance we had come to the conclusion that this was not the right solution for us. Although there is a certain charm and also a certain logic about developing a museum based on one's own home, where the collection has been built up, we firmly rejected this option. The main reason was that in our opinion quite different requirements apply to a museum, with respect to lighting, visitor processing, internal transport (we have always collected sculptures!) and so on, than to a home built for a totally different purpose. And alterations, supplemented with new structures, nearly always lead to compromises and to combinations of different styles that are hardly a cause for admiration. So we arrived almost inevitably at the idea of a new building. This decision was thus based on a mixture of efficiency considerations and aesthetic views. Our many museum visits had already helped convince us that we had a pretty good idea of what we did and did not want. As to the latter: in many places we had seen that even in brand-new museums too little consideration had been given to the specific requirements (lighting, transport) of a sculpture museum. What is more, we had seen quite a number of highly praised museum buildings which seemed to us to be first and foremost monuments to the architect concerned and which exhibited a lack of functionality.

The choice of Quist

Like the decision to build anew, the choice of architect was based on both practical and aesthetic considerations. Both considerations are a reflection of personal inclination, of individual preferences.

As to the practical side: I do not believe in architects who have no eye for the efficiency of a building, in particular for such aspects as durability and maintenance. This perspective weighs so heavily with me that on my first visit to the Pompidou Centre, for example, I never got around to considering its possible beauty because I judged it a maintenance disaster. Nor do I have much time for master-architects who pay scant attention to the costs of a building and, to some extent related to this, do not guide and monitor the construction process adequately. On the aesthetic side, the important thing is that my wife and I, certainly when it comes to a museum, both prefer simplicity in architecture.

The choice of Wim Quist becomes clearer in the light of the above. We had seen several of his works and I had been told that he was not a big spender and that he supervised the construction effectively. Another factor in Quist's favour was that he had already built several museums; he did not need to invent the wheel. This emphasis on the practical aspects should not be misunderstood: we would never have chosen Quist had we not first and foremost been captivated by his architecture.

One factor that played no role at all was Quist the man. We did not know him, nor did

we bother to make inquiries about him. In fact this was a bit careless of us, for building
a museum for your own collection is comparable to building your own home and the
question of whether you get along with your architect is obviously far from unimportant.
It will quite probably influence the result and it will very definitely influence the proces of
getting there, the personal experience of the development process. You build a museum
only once in your life and you do it for your enjoyment. Besides, my wife and I – at any rate,
together – were actually interested in every aspect of the museum business. We had (and
have) opinions about display techniques, about space, lighting, pedestals, about subsidiary
facilities like the museum shop and café, and – no less important – about the running of a
museum: the position and quality of the staff, the contact with the visitors, provision of
information, and so on. There are museum founders who make their collection available
and furnish the money for a building to house it. That is in itself a great deal. But our
ambitions went even further than this and so it was only to be expected that, given all
these aspirations on our side, there would be additional demands on the personal aspect
of the collaboration with the architect.

There is one other point that should be mentioned here in explaining the choice of
architect. The idea of building a museum does not stop with a plan. It is the realization
that matters. Well then, in the Netherlands in the second half of the twentieth century,
in virtually every building project of any significance, dream and deed are separated by a
host of obstacles: authorities with divergent opinions, obstructive neighbours and other
concerned parties. And they all wallow in an overabundance of legislation aimed at giving
maximum scope to caution and judicial bodies that are consequently swamped with work.
The eleven years that separated dream and deed in our case taught this client that here,
too, the choice of architect is crucial. That was something else we did not know when
we made our choice. Inexperience, in other words.

The beginning

At our first meeting, Quist asked whether we had ever seen any museums that came
close to our ideal. A very practical question, because if, for example, we had replied, yes,
Pompidou, or (if the discussion had taken place twenty years later) Groningen, we need
have gone no further. Our answer was: yes indeed and in two places. One is the
Glyptothek in Munich, the other Louis Kahn's Kimbell Art Museum in Fort Worth (this
virtually unknown metropolis is a twin city of the very well-known Dallas). We had just
come back from visiting the Kimball Museum and were still full of it. I shall never forget
how Wim Quist's face lit up at that moment. We shall probably be able to get along then,
he observed, and told us of his enormous admiration for Kahn and for this museum in
particular. He had even visited it during construction in order to watch it take shape.

He also, of course, asked about the nature of our collection. We did not need many words to describe it: sculpture, made during the second half of the twentieth century, focusing on the human image in the broad sense. Ranging in style from highly abstract to detailed figurative, with a great variation as to country of origin and materials. An important aspect in our discussion was of course the size of the sculptures. We indicated that our measure was the human measure and that we wanted to stick to that principle both in later additions to the collection and in exhibitions of work from outside.

This principle was by no means self-evident. In various museum collections, whether displayed indoors or outside in sculpture gardens, there was a noticeable trend towards very large dimensions. In view of our collection and its theme, but also in view of the available space, this was certainly not a trend we wished to follow.

The building programme

The book in which this essay appears is about the Beelden aan Zee Museum in Scheveningen. Our original intention, however, had been to build the museum in Bilthoven. That was where we were then living, where we had a sufficiently large plot of land and where we also had a number of friends and acquaintances whom we planned to involve in the scheme one way or another. We had called the house where we were living 'The Unfinished' (De Onvoltooide in Dutch). It stood on Schubert Avenue, I admired and sang many of this composer's *Lieder* and a house is never finished, either literally or figuratively – hence the name. The museum was to bear the same name.

After many years' endeavour, the plan for a museum in Bilthoven had to be abandoned and the choice fell, almost by accident, on Scheveningen. How this came about I shall not go into here. But it is appropriate in a discussion of the relationship with Quist to pursue the argument with respect to Bilthoven. For this reason I shall first mention the building programme as formulated for De Onvoltooide, and then indicate the changes that were introduced when Scheveningen became the location.

De Onvoltooide

I Object
Design of museum and garden

II Specifications
A
1 Function geared mainly to sculpture; possibility of exhibiting paintings/graphic art;

2 Premises for additional functions:
– library/study area
– shop
– café
– office
– lecture room/conference room
– studio
3 Living accommodation, consisting of
– small dwelling for security guard
– small flat for temporary residence (living/bed/bath/kitchen)
B
Overall plan, based on available site; phased implementation
C
Museum open only during 'extended' summer, but to be fitted out so that it can be heated
throughout at a later date; subsidiary premises (reading room, library, café) and living
accommodation suitable for use in winter.

III Starting points
1 Complete unity of indoor plan and outdoor plan by means of styling (buildings, awnings,
fencing, patios, pergolas) and materials.
2 Buildings, pergolas, etc. to be located and styled in such a way as to
– facilitate orientation, e.g. with respect to exit
– allow for efficient routing for visitors
– satisfy ambience requirements for subsidiary premises
3 Simple, classic, timeless styling
4 Use of a small number of well-tried, highly durable, low-maintenance and inexpensive materials
(and plantings)
5 Simple construction techniques
6 Maximum exploitation of natural light, with simple corrective option

Thus far, an exact rendering of the building programme I drew up for Bilthoven. Any
further clarification seems to me unnecessary. This complete statement serves merely
to indicate what our role as client, vis-à-vis the architect, actually entailed.[1]

In the early contacts with the architect, in particular, you have the feeling that you are setting out on some kind of an adventure. You have spent a long time thinking about it and now you are entering unfamiliar territory. You do it for the end result but in my case I was also attracted by the process of getting there. In this slightly euphoric mood, my wife and I sent Wim Quist a rhyming New Year's greeting at the end of 1986. In translation it goes something like this:

a dream we did share
of a home for the sculptures
then questions appeared
of who? how? and where?
if the where is 'right here'
and the who is 'Wim Quist'
that's two done for a start
only how's still to chart
but Quist thought (at year's end)
when all's said and done:
in the beginning was the plan

Yet the making of the plan was not all smooth sailing. One reason was certainly that the shape of the available plot did not make for a logical and elegant ordering of the various functions. But a more important reason was the less than perfect harmony on the personal front. Why was the collaboration not working? Was it his fault, was it my fault? There is a saying that 'it takes two to make a quarrel'. Perhaps so, but that was not the problem in this case. At issue here was the role of client and that of architect and this in turn raised the question of their respective authority. Of course, character also plays a part in such matters and on top of this, Quist's domestic situation (his wife's illness) was a cause of worry to him during almost the entire eleven-year period of our collaboration. However, the way I saw it, and still see it, the cause lay chiefly with me.

I was, as I've already said, interested in architecture; I had strong opinions on the subject and what is more, I had gradually formed a clear picture of how the projected museum should look. Apart from the fact that the building programme itself contained a firm diktat, I was not averse to putting my oar in now and then. What I really wanted was to guide Quist's hand a bit and as it happened he was having none of it. Driving back after a visit to his home to discuss the problem that had arisen, I realized that I would have to choose. Either play the architect myself to some extent and work with someone who would follow my promptings, or submit to a real architect whom we had chosen because of his proven excellence. When it came down to it, I had little difficulty choosing the latter option and for my wife this was the right decision. I fancy that I also made my choice clear in my subsequent demeanour. Seldom, as I came to realize, have I been so well rewarded for a fundamental surrender, and on three fronts. In the first place because the collaboration was a pleasure from that moment onward, and the importance of this aspect became even clearer when we had to endure together the many difficulties I referred to above, first in Bilthoven and later again in Scheveningen. In the second place because I am convinced that the result has turned out much better than anything that would have emerged from a collaboration with a 'willing' architect. And in the third place because Wim Quist nonetheless gave us plenty of opportunity to have our own say, so that I am confident that while the architecture is entirely Quist's, our participation was such that the pleasurable sense of 'our own museum' has a genuine basis in fact. Of course, another important element, apart from the latitude people allow one another in a successful collaboration, is that our views on taste frequently coincided.

Scheveningen

When Bilthoven proved to be unfeasible and Scheveningen entered the picture, the building programme was reformulated. We did not have to think twice about asking Quist again. In accepting, he mentioned among other things that he considered the light in this place by the sea to be unique – and he referred to the painters of The Hague School who had evidently also been fascinated by that light – and furthermore that he regarded it as a challenge to create a completely different atmosphere from the one that prevails, especially in summer, along the rest of the Boulevard.
The new building programme read as follows:

Building programme for museum in Scheveningen

The building programme remains essentially unchanged with the following annotations.

General
There is – in the form of the Pavilion[2] – a built accommodation already in place; it should be investigated whether, and if so what, possibilities exist for joint exploitation of spaces currently used by 'De Witte' (the owner of the Pavilion).

sub II A3

a modest living space for the security guard, based on his present accommodation, is desirable here as well; a small apartment is of course unnecessary (NB we were then living nearby in a large apartment)

sub III

The starting points remain more or less the same, although there is now the Pavilion as an additional, dominant starting point. For the rest, the steps and plateaus – those going down from Gevers Deynootweg to the Pavilion – are an interesting given.

Thus the text, as I then formulated it.

There is quite a big difference between this building programme and the museum as realized. That is because the programme was written when the idea of the new site first arose and Quist had been asked to investigate the possibilities. As soon as we had walked around in the Pavilion together we realized that the possibilities for using the Pavilion for museum purposes – and that in collaboration with 'De Witte' – were minimal. The upstairs spaces are on a modest scale; the cellars are low-ceilinged and receive scarcely any natural light. It soon became clear that the museum would have to be an entirely new structure alongside the Pavilion. No new building programme was drawn up at this point. Nor was one necessary, for during the (five) years we had spent working with Quist on the Bilthoven project, he had of course become completely familiar with our views.

There are several reasons why the building programme drawn up for Bilthoven clearly differs from the realized museum on a number of points. Firstly, some parts of the programme for Bilthoven were unnecessary in Scheveningen (living space) or impossible, or less appropriate (a studio); conversely, some of the restrictions applying to the plan for Bilthoven were not retained for Scheveningen (opening for only part of the year). Secondly, our views and our options had changed somewhat.

And finally, in some instances the same specifications resulted in a different choice. Whereas for the wooded site in Bilthoven, for example, the chosen construction material had been brick, for the rampart-like situation in Scheveningen both parties were agreed that concrete was the obvious choice.

The design for Beelden aan Zee

In contrast to Bilthoven, the draft design for Scheveningen was fairly quickly committed to paper. The realization of the museum, however, took several more years. Not only because here, too, legal proceedings against the museum as such caused delay. But also because, unlike in Bilthoven, where the design had met with very little criticism, there were quite significant difficulties in The Hague during the design stage. The initially unforeseen demands of the Delfland District Water Control Board regarding the retention of sand for the benefit of the sea wall, had far-reaching consequences for the design, resulting in the ascending terraces on the south side and a retaining wall around the entire site. The local planning authority also had its say, albeit a confusing say. Some of the members felt that the museum volume manifested itself too strongly vis à vis the Pavilion, others felt that it did not manifest itself strongly enough. The practical consequence was that Quist replaced the proposed concrete roof with a steel one, thus making it possible to obtain greater internal height within the permitted total height.

Because of the Water Control Board's demands, the design turned out a lot more expensive, but fortunately also finer. It is typical of Quist's attitude that he became very worried about the total investment costs during these developments and suggested that we have a preliminary investment estimate drawn up. We followed his advice, of course; fortunately he turned out to have been too pessimistic.

I should like to make clear that the design in its realized form is entirely Quist's. We exerted no influence whatever over it, nor did we feel any need to do so. We were, however, involved in various aspects of the implementation: the colour of the concrete – to match the sand in the dunes – was at our request, the sand-coloured granite floor we selected in Italy, the timber for the ceilings and the stainless steel 'studs' in the concrete walls were our choice as regards material. But there was of course proper consultation on each element of choice. Moreover, Quist decided on the method of application and in particular the dimensions. And to avoid any misunderstanding: he rejected some of my suggestions and was no doubt right to do so.

Nowadays, in the construction of larger, complex projects, the architect is assisted by a structural engineer. The latter's role is quite properly discussed in the essay dealing with the structural aspects of Beelden aan Zee. Quist often works with bureau ABT in Velp. There are undoubtedly big advantages in working with a more or less permanent 'partner'; you understand one another, start to speak the same language and to complement one another. Quist's sparring partner on this project was Rob Nijsse. It is my belief that he made a significant contribution on all kinds of technical matters relating to design and execution. Apart from his professional expertise, his clear-headedness and pleasant personality certainly played an important role in this.

Interior

Many famous master-architects, from Palladio to Mies van der Rohe, were of the opinion that when they designed a building, the design of the interior was also their task. I think this is a very valid point of view; we too were inclined towards a 'Gesamtkunstwerk'. It was not until construction work had begun, although early enough to allow for delivery times, that we took the decision to invite Quist to design the interior as well: showcases, cloakroom, furniture, bookcases for the library, museum shop and office. He reacted very positively indeed. I noticed that he worked on this with almost greater enthusiasm than on the design for the building. Which was also very agreeable for us, since my wife and I were once again closely involved in this aspect.

Evaluation

So far I have been mainly concerned to describe the division of roles and the relationship with the architect. To this I should now like to append an evaluation. In so doing I shall also consider the various phases of our collaboration.

During the design phase I was struck by a remarkable duality in Quist's character. On the one hand one notices in contacts with him that he does not think primarily in terms of money and that, for example, he does not have certain prices (cubic metre of concrete, square metre of brickwork) at his fingertips; and one certainly notices that he is not 'commercially minded', that he is not out to enrich himself. On the other hand he is continually making remarks like: have you any idea of the costs, it can surely be done more simply and cheaper; he exhibits an unremitting concern for the budget. If there is any trace of luxury in Beelden aan Zee, it is definitely not down to Quist but must certainly be attributed to us, the client. Anyone familiar with my origins, career and inclinations will understand that this combination of qualities was highly gratifying to me.

Another observation. As I have already mentioned, during the design phase in particular, my wife and I always conducted the consultations with Quist together. During these many discussions I noted with appreciation that he paid at least as much attention to the little my wife said as he did to my considerably lengthier interventions.

Control during the implementation phase, is of course finely balanced. Day-to-day control – on behalf of the architect – was in our case exercised by an independent person, but someone Quist knew well and who was also retained at his suggestion. All the (usually weekly) building meetings were led by a capable member of Quist's staff whith whom he had been cooperating for over twenty-five years. Whenever Quist joined us and also during consultations about implementation matters between times, I was always struck by his respectful manner towards the contractor and his people. Conversely – and this is hardly surprising: the one elicits the other – the same was true. The supervisors listened to his opinion and gave it due consideration.

All construction jobs, and certainly the more complex building projects, have to contend with unforeseen incidents and surprises. Here, too, the task was not a simple one.

As a result of the site and partly fortuitous weather conditions, the builders were often faced with well-nigh insoluble problems. Pouring concrete in a force 7 wind, on the coast, is no sinecure. On top of this there was the notorious problem concerning the physical link-up between the new building and the old Pavilion. This was a real setback and could easily have lead to tensions. Quist is not someone who hides behind an excuse in such situations, instead he tackles the problem in a calm and collected manner, in particular by meticulously reviewing possible solutions. And in this way we managed to get through the difficulties occasionally thrown up by the construction process.

Between the design and implementation phases lay the longest period, which I shall simply call the procedural phase. In our case it was a particularly long period because it encompassed two projects, Bilthoven and Scheveningen. The events of this phase, too, taught me to appreciate Quist for his personal qualities. It was not the happiest period of our building history. We, as the initiators, came in for a lot of criticism. But Quist had to put up with a great deal more. From insolent laymen, who – a curious by-product of our 'open', give-everyone-a-say society – were too often given every opportunity to air their insults. And from colleagues, sometimes even virtual nonentities, whose implicit or explicit arrogance just has to be tolerated. For that one has become a universally respected and experienced architect? Quist is a sensitive man and such usage does not leave him unaffected. But he is also a dignified man. He does not browbeat his audience, nor does he resort to sophistry or clever remarks. He explains his ideas calmly and clearly and impresses those who are prepared to listen as honourable and circumspect. I am glad that a man of this stamp, with this personality, was looking after our interests during this taxing, but unavoidable phase.

It stands to reason that a client's evaluation of an architect should culminate in what the architect finally achieves. Since its completion, some hundreds of thousands of people have visited Beelden aan Zee and dozens of them, professionals and amateurs, ordinary and erudite, have sung the building's praises. Naturally it gives us pleasure to hear this. But in the end one's value judgements are dictated by one's own taste. In our opinion Beelden aan Zee stands for truth and character in architecture. It is more handsome than we had even dared to hope. The collaboration between this client and this architect was a pleasure that had to begin hesitantly. Quist had to stand firm in order to be able to manipulate form, function and construction for the benefit of the objective, in this instance a museum. The writer of this reflection had to discover that Quist could not be a complaisant man because he is an honest architect.

Theo Scholten

54

1
For the garden section of the museum we consulted with landscape architect Jan Boon, from 't Goy/Houten, who had already designed a substantial portion of our private garden.
2
The Pavilion originally was built (1827) as a summer day-residence for the then Dutch queen.

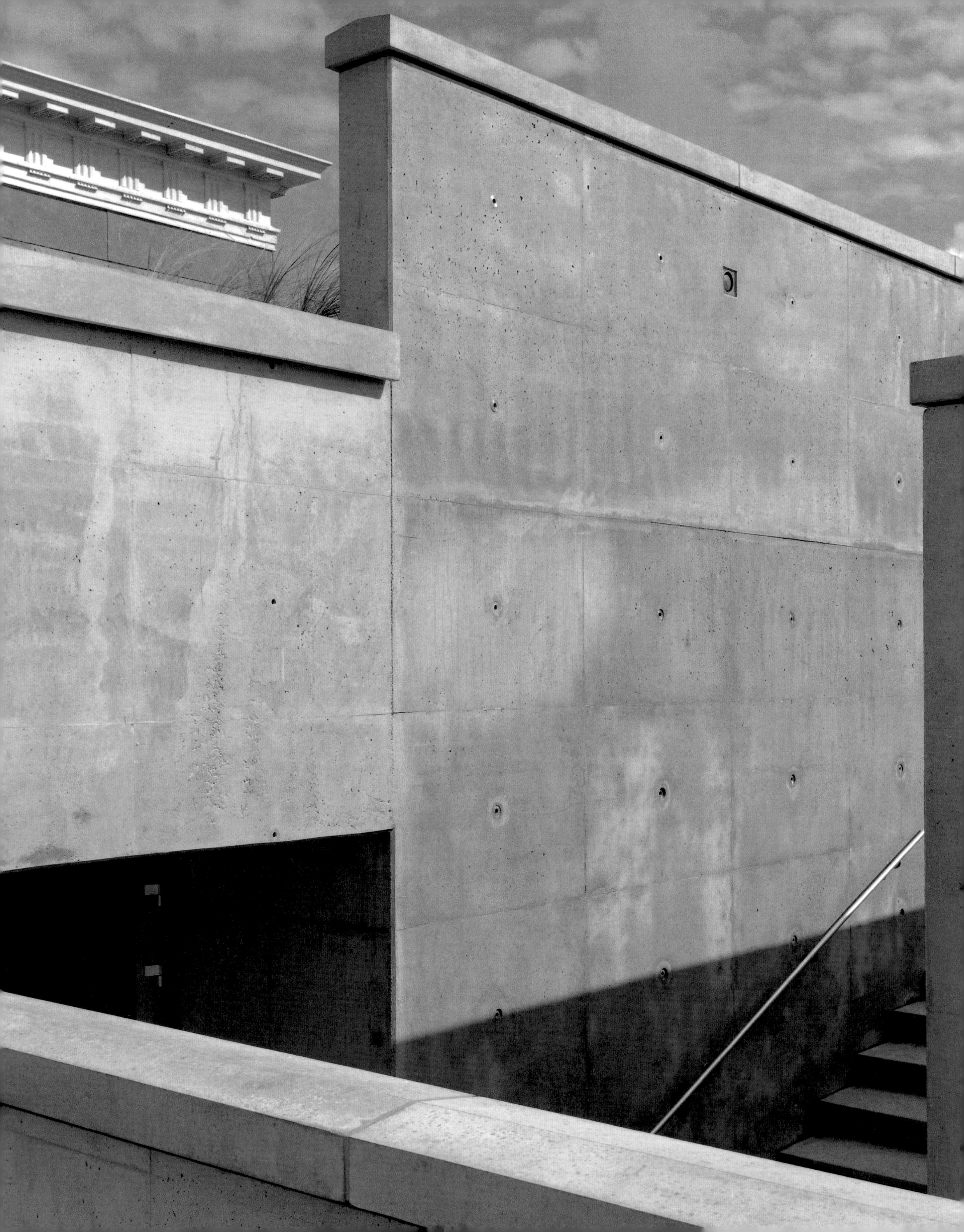

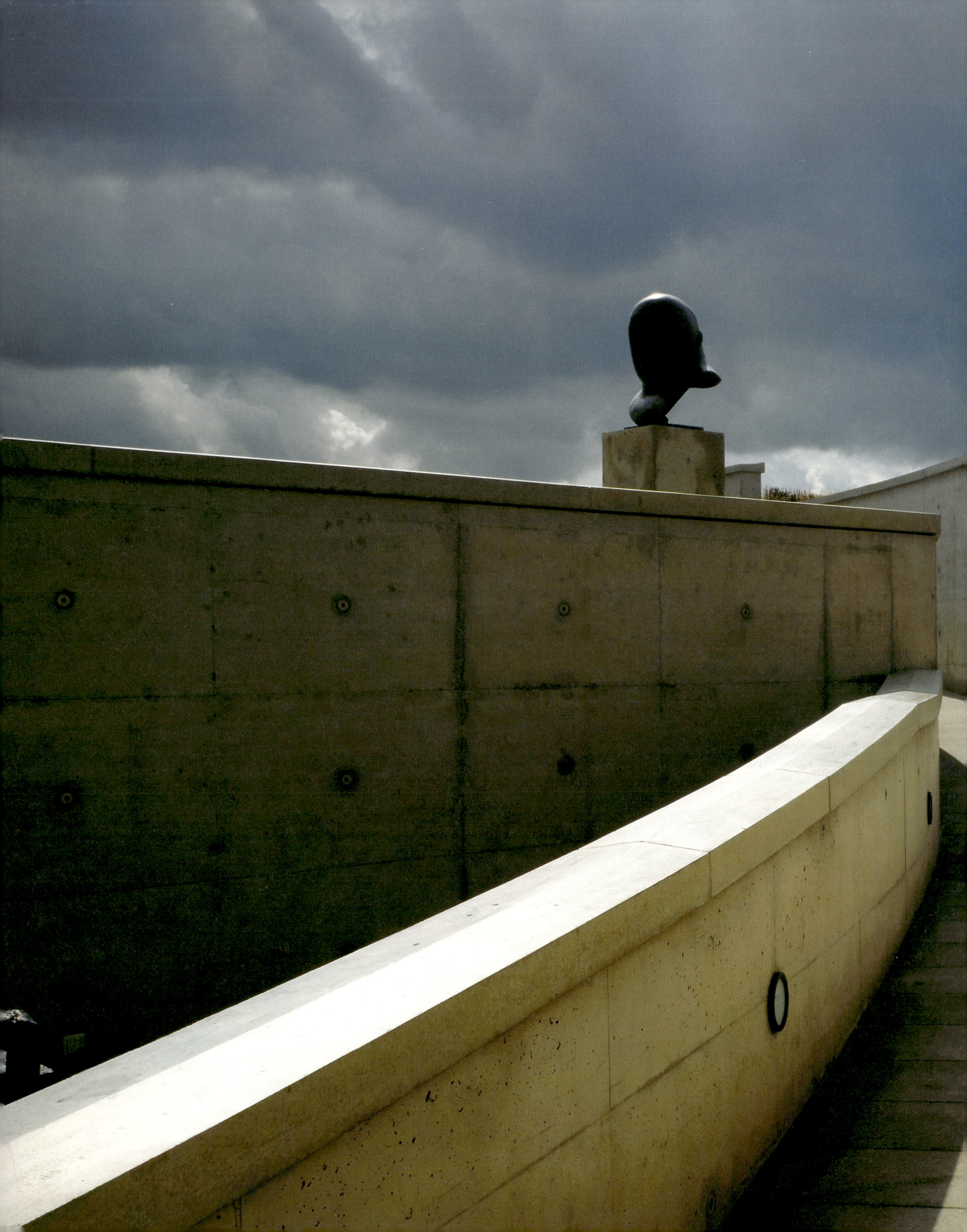

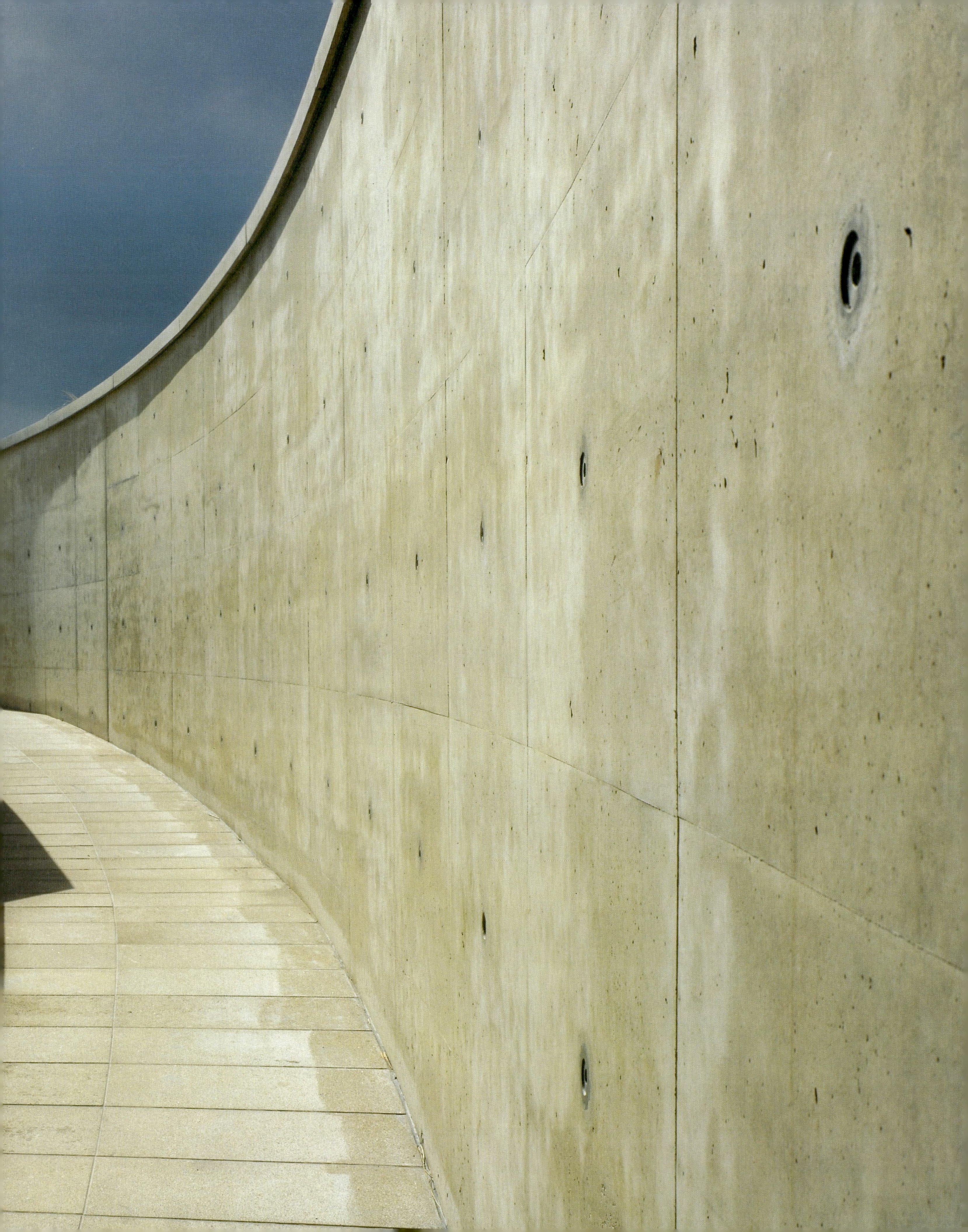

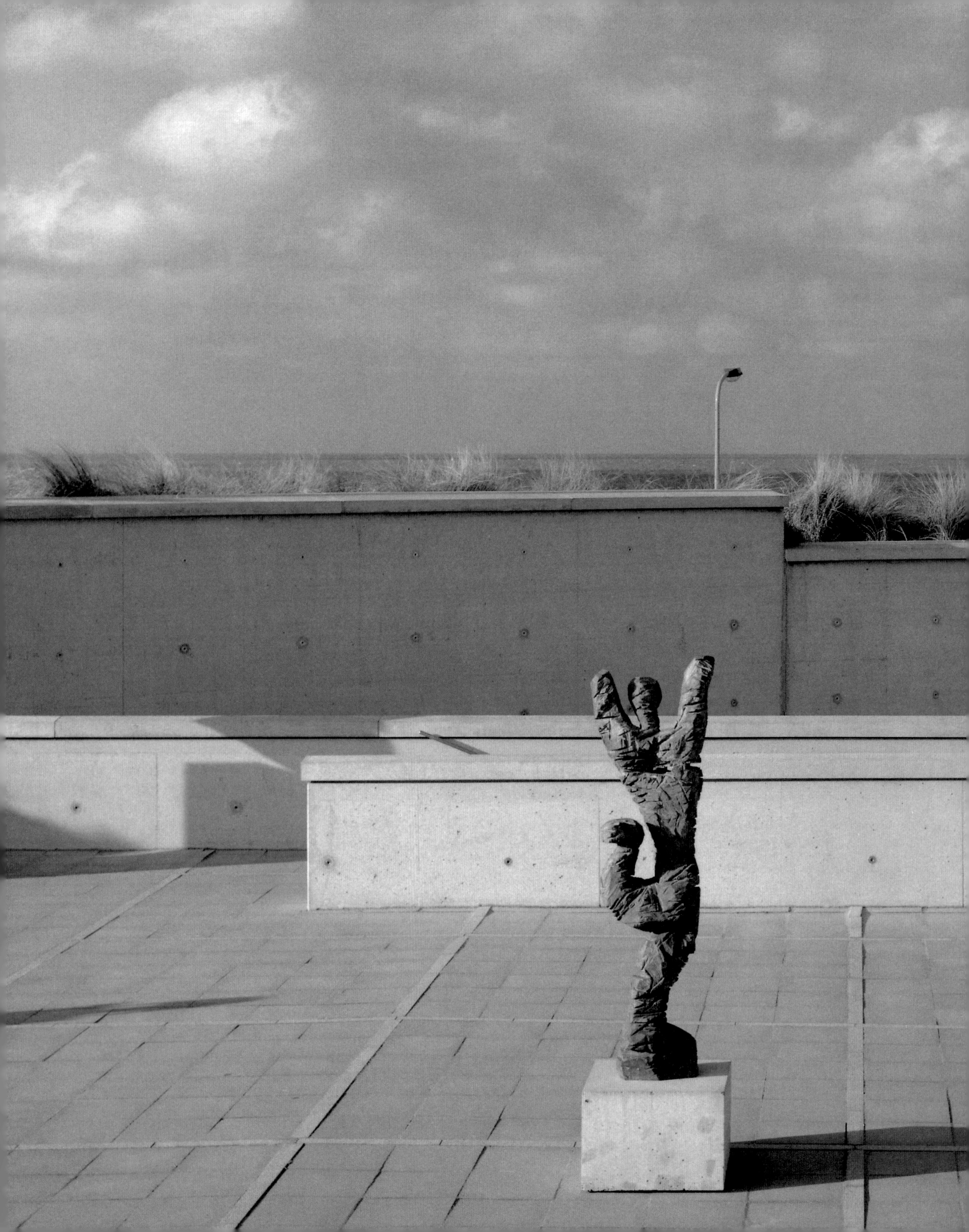

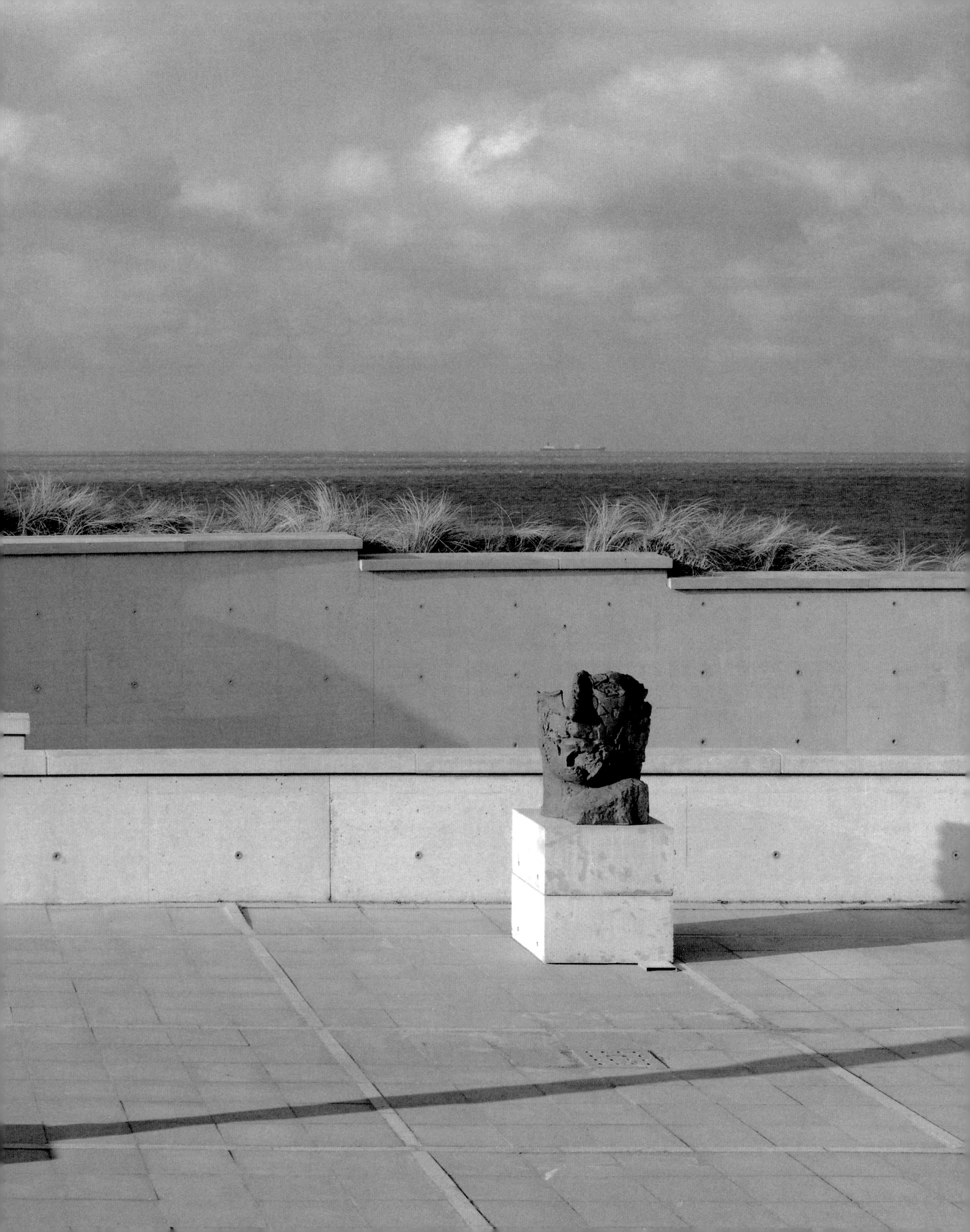

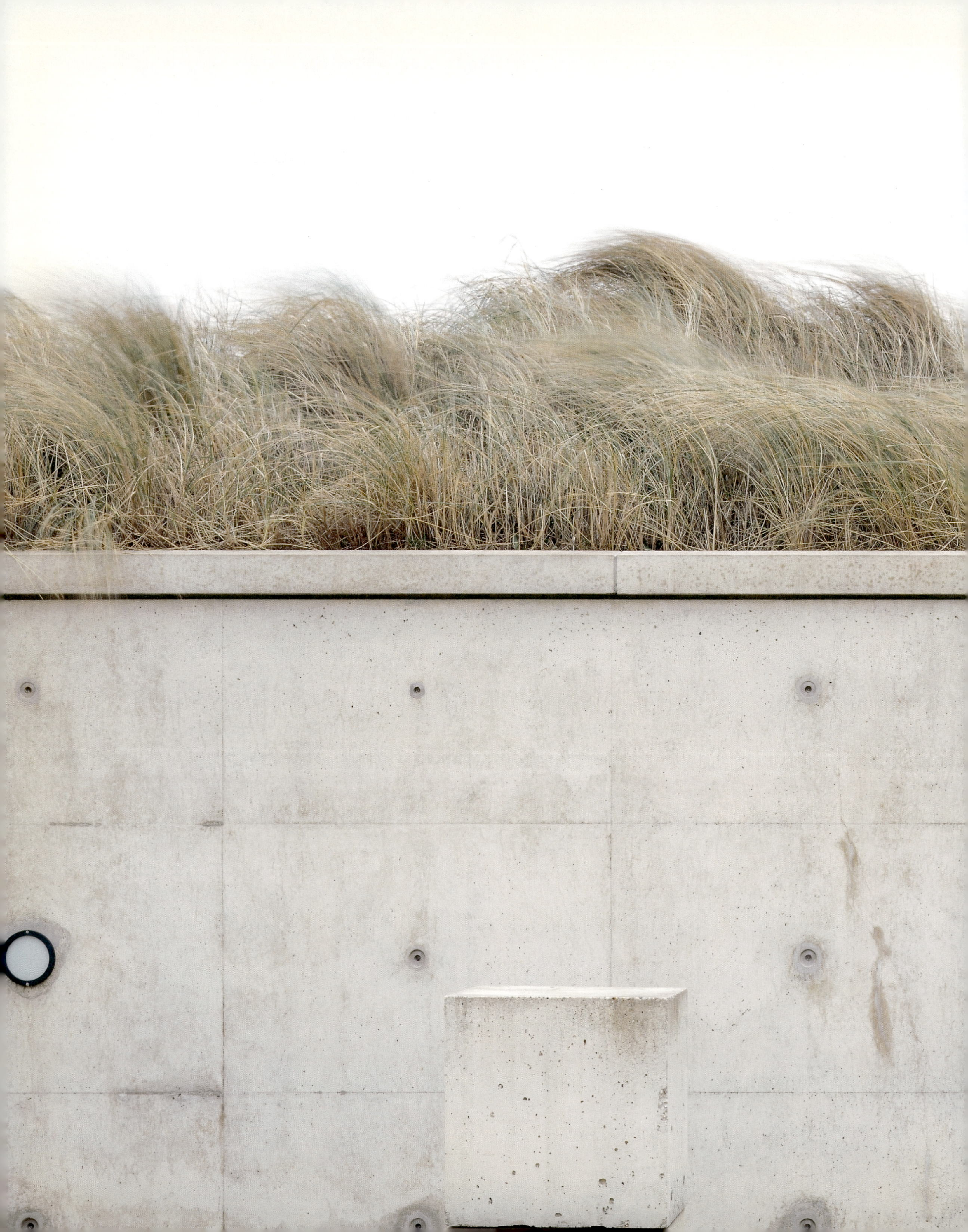

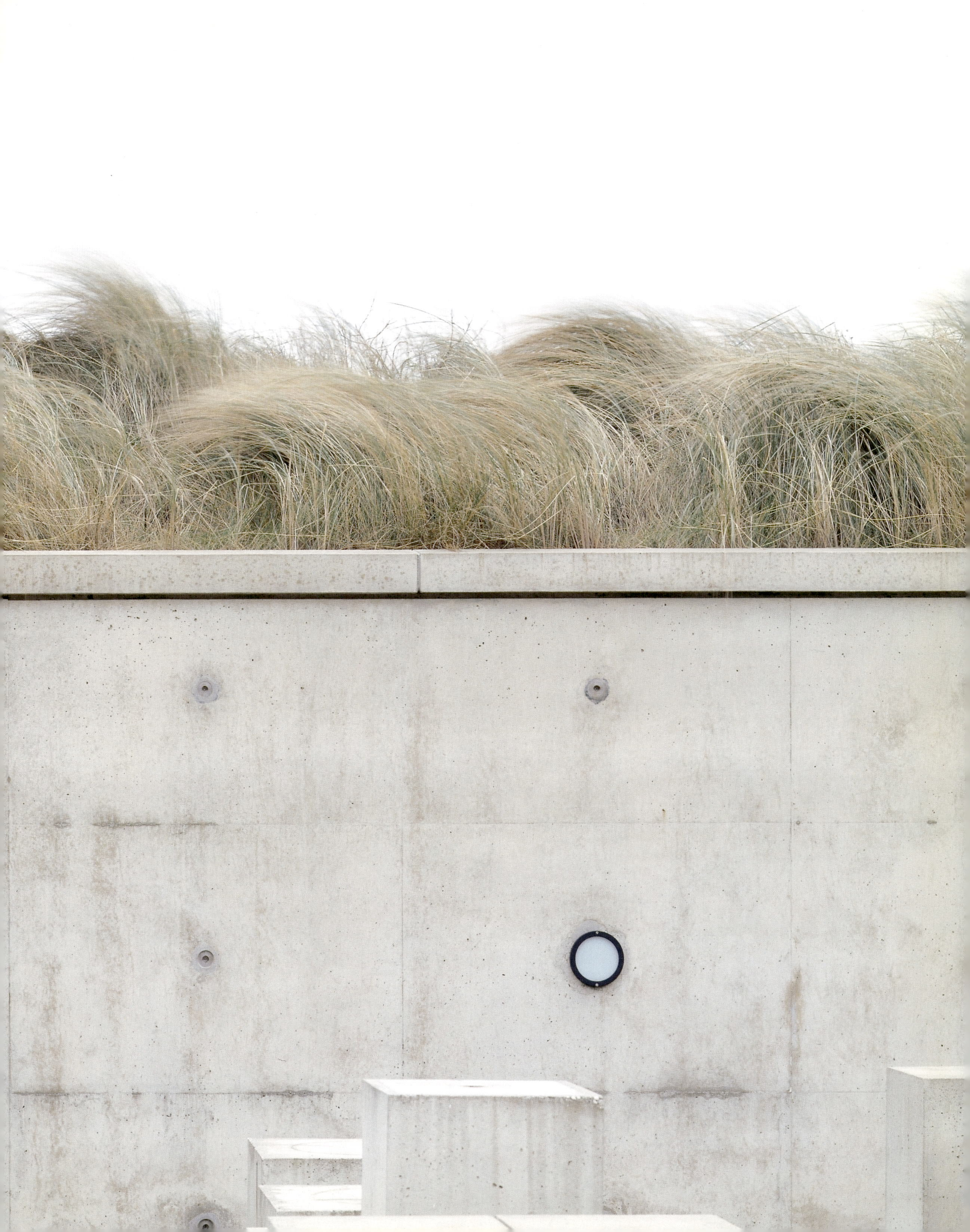

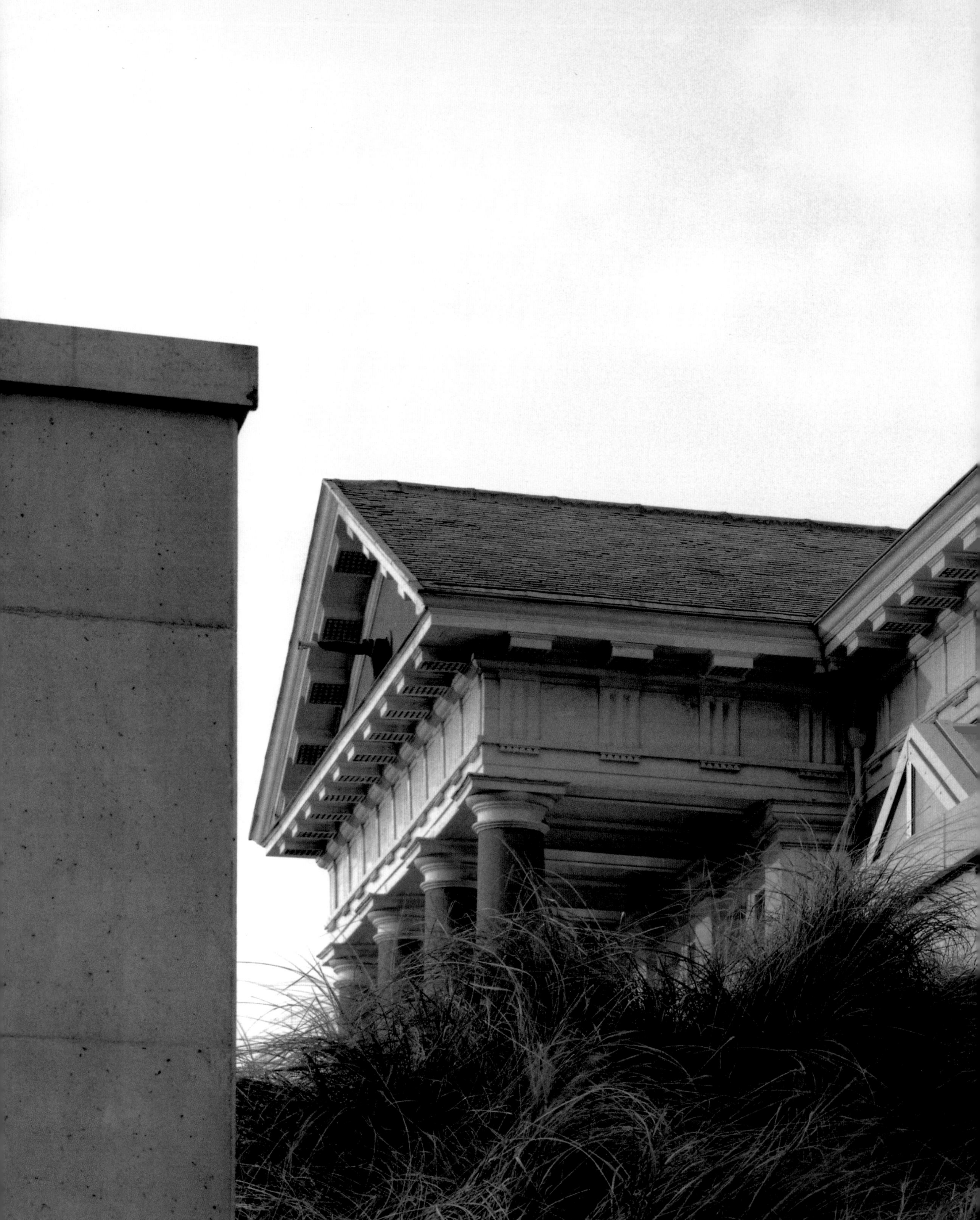

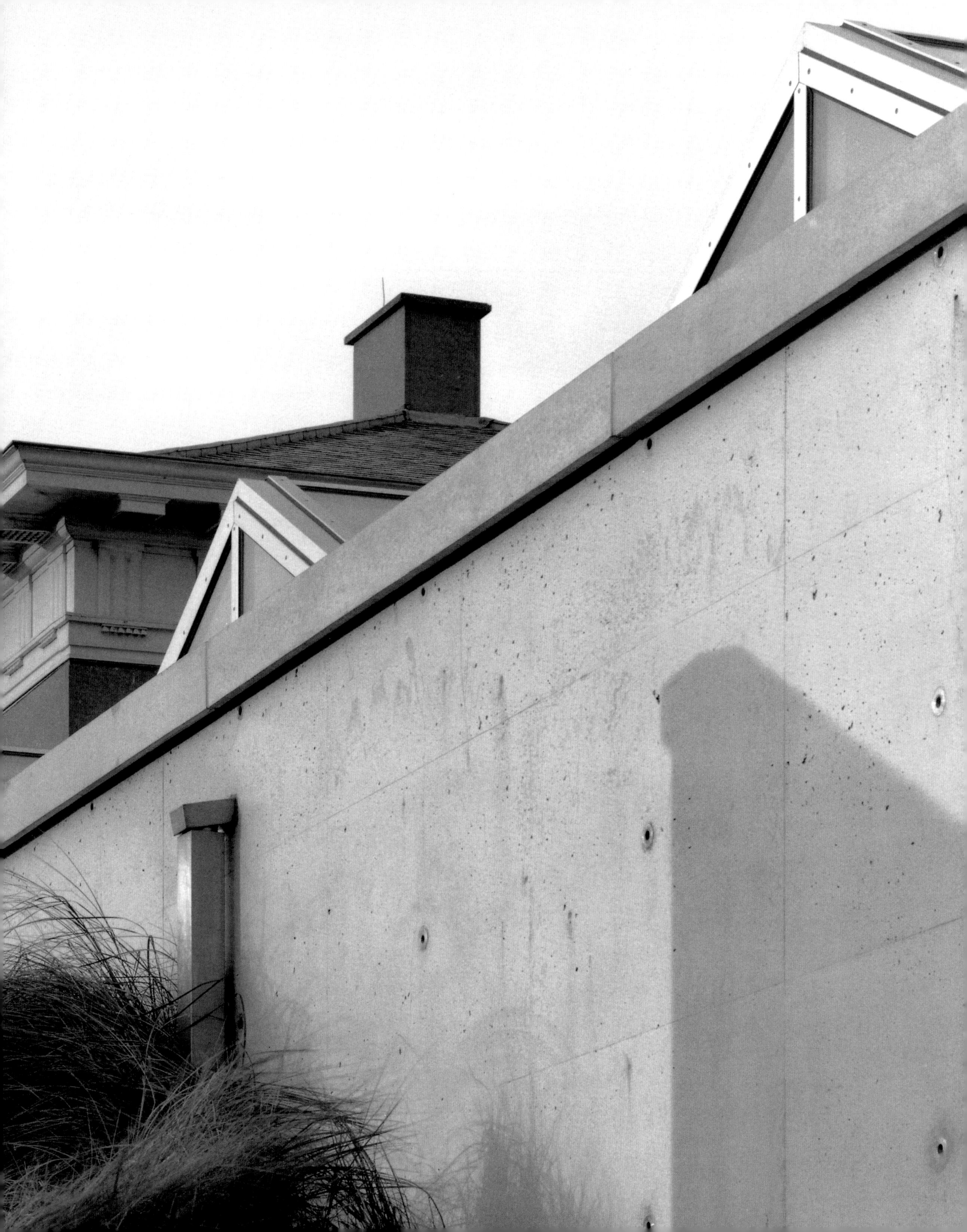

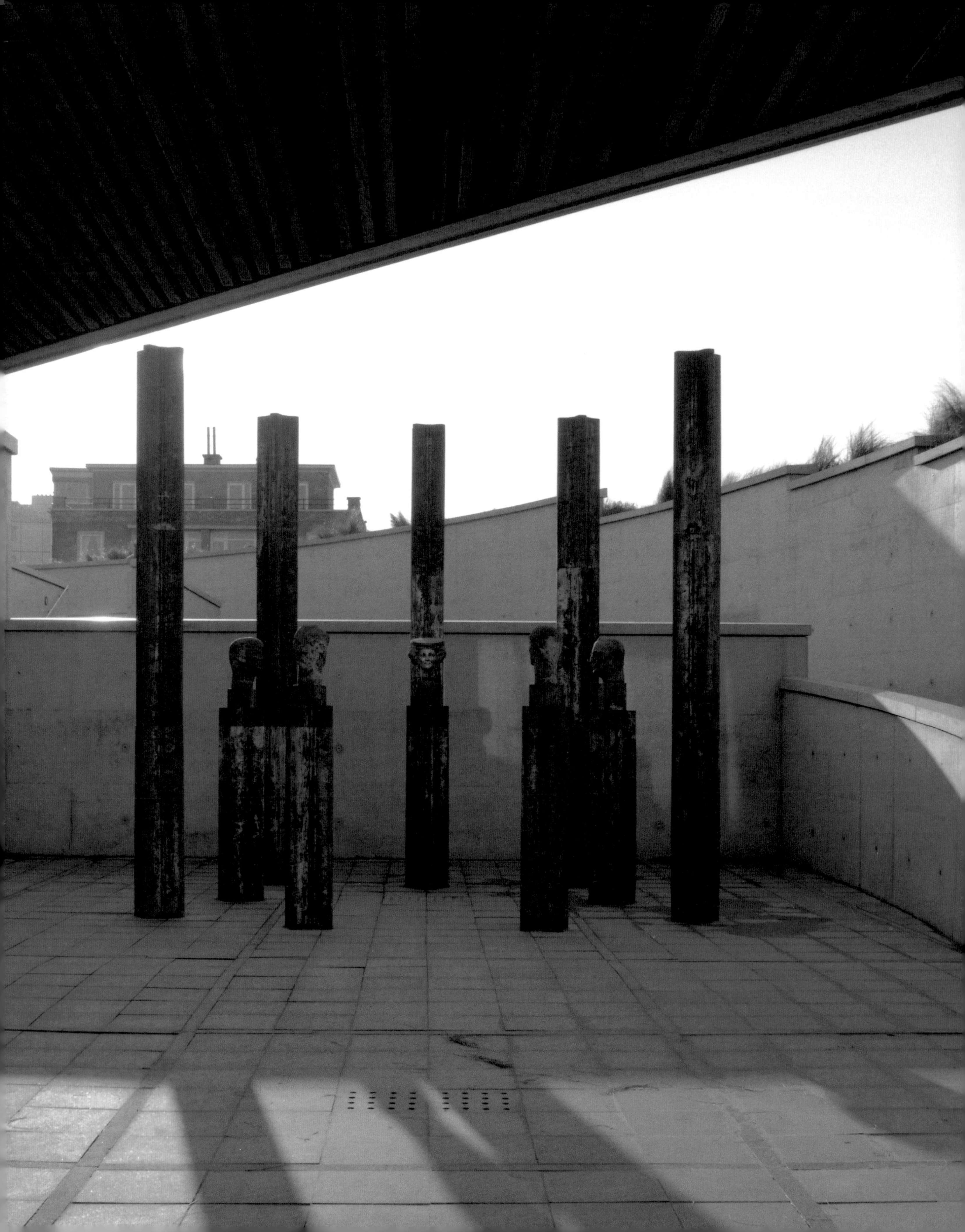

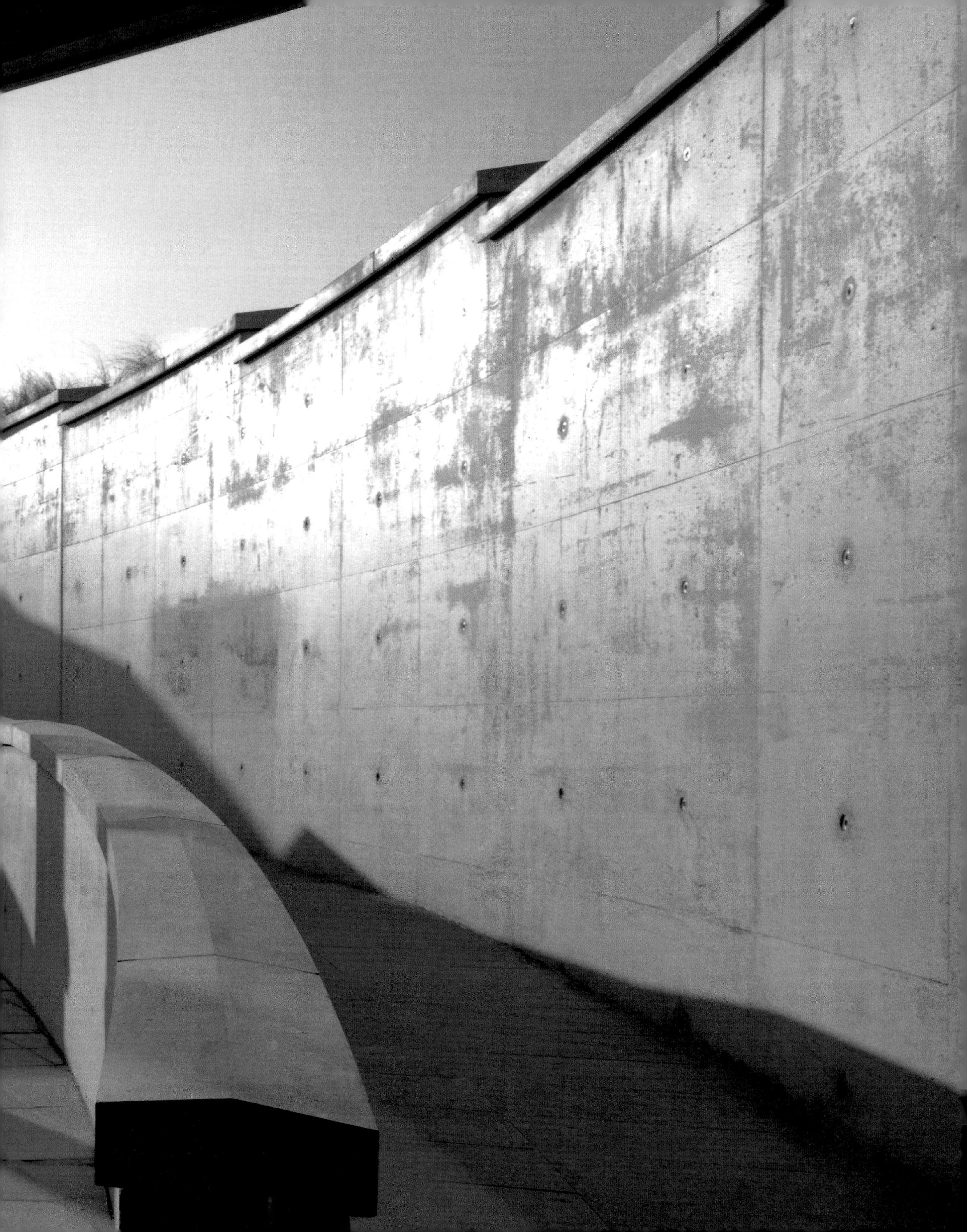

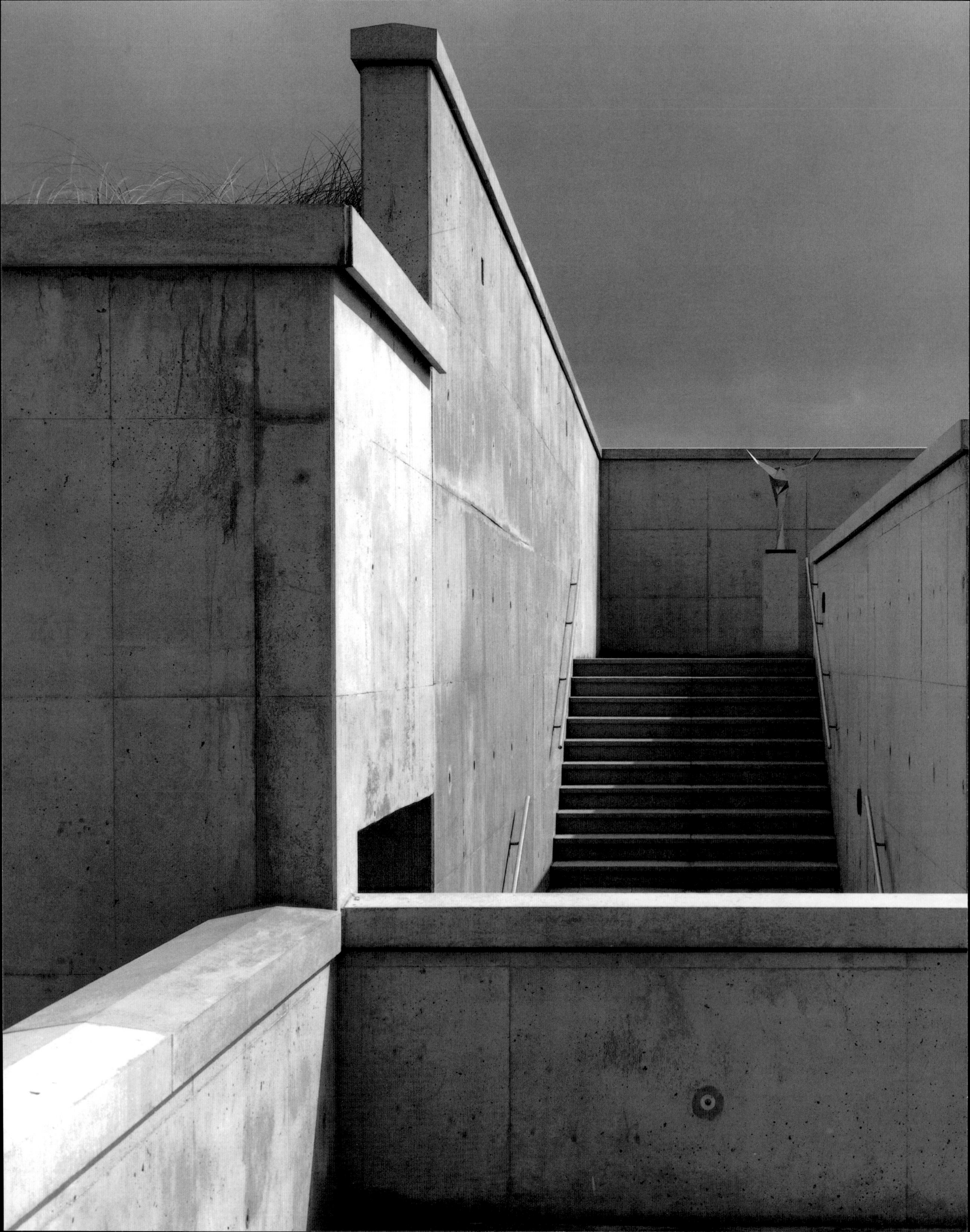

A building in a sand dune

The commission

In 1989, after earlier plans for the construction of a museum to house the Scholten-Miltenburg collection in Bilthoven had come to naught, the choice of location fell on Scheveningen: to be precise, on the last stretch of dune-land between Harteveltstraat and Jongeneelstraat, some 140 metres long and 70 metres wide. This location was not without its problems. In the middle of the dune stands the Von Wied pavilion, built in 1826 at the behest of King Willem I for his wife, Wilhelmina of Prussia. The pavilion is a listed building and belongs to a Hague-based literary society, 'De Witte', which uses it as a summer annexe. The area around the pavilion had to remain free; that was the wish of the client but also of the local residents who were opposed to any building on or raising of the dune. Given the limited size of the location, this meant that the new building should impact as little as possible on the outward appearance of the dune. The logical solution would have been to bury the museum completely in the ground, had it not been for the fact that the dune forms part of the primary sea defence. The body responsible for managing this, the Hoogheemraadschap Delfland (Delfland Water Control Board), initially insisted that not a single cubic metre of sand should be removed from the dune. After extensive studies, which also entailed calling in outside experts, a compromise was reached: a crucial link in the sea wall right next to the dune could be reinforced by using 3500 m³ dune sand from the building site to raise the level of a car park beside the boulevard. For the rest, not one grain of sand was to be removed from the site, not even temporarily during construction.

    The architect Wim Quist, who had also been involved in the plans for Bilthoven, was asked to produce a design. The client had chosen Quist primarily because of his excellent track record as a museum architect, but Quist has also had considerable experience with civil engineering works. And while the Beelden aan Zee Museum is not a

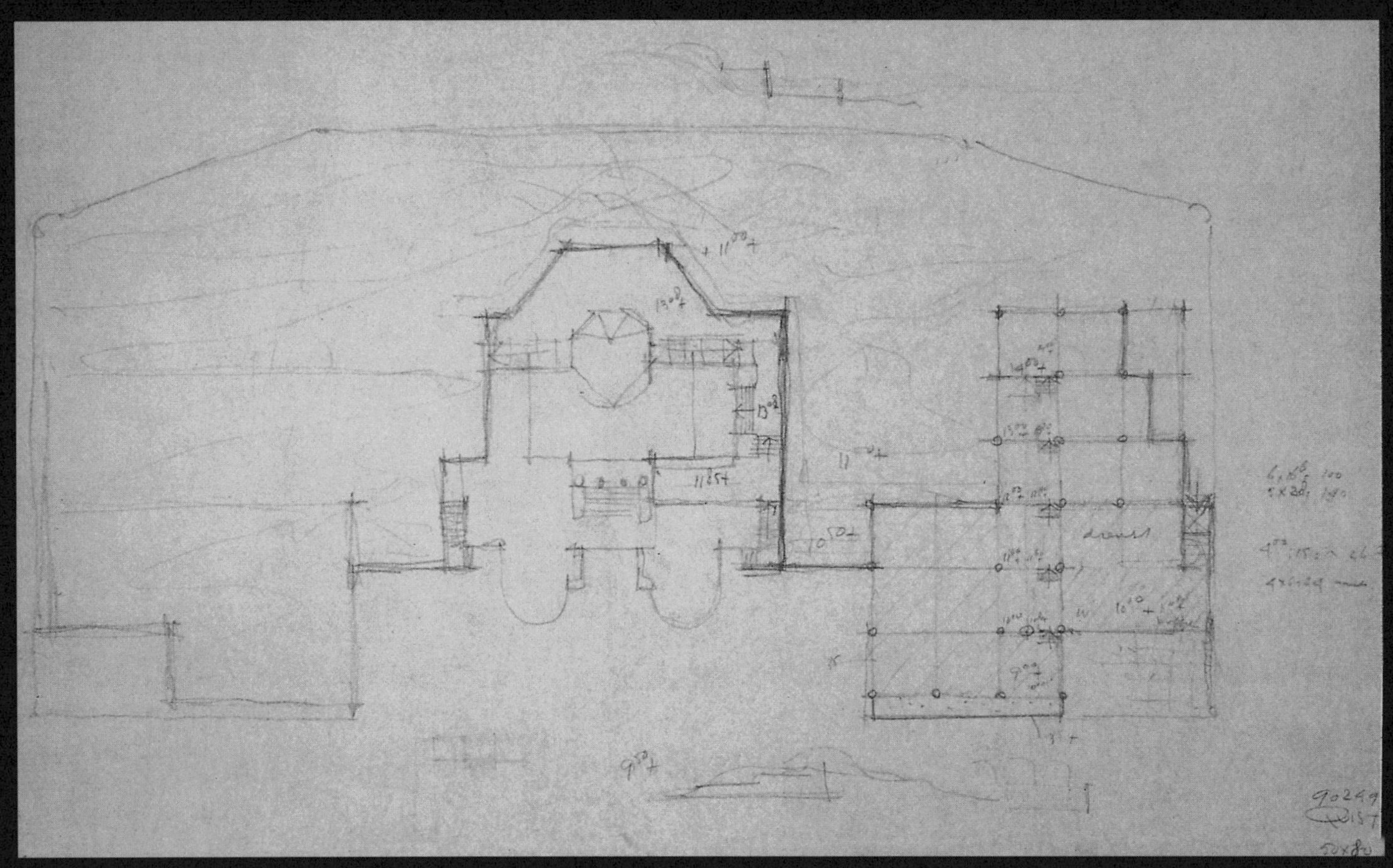

true civil engineering work, the sober and sturdy materials and design that characterize much of Quist's work and which also fit in with the ideas of Mr and Mrs Scholten, are entirely appropriate to a half-buried structure entailing the containment of many metres of sand, and an aggressive coastal environment.

Design

Because the pavilion is situated exactly in the middle of the dune and a site covering only half the total surface area would have offered too few possibilities, there was nothing for it but to build the museum on either side of the pavilion with a connecting passage running below or at the foot of the pavilion. This determined the level of the museum.

Quist gave the pavilion a central place in his design and for the boundary of the museum on the seaward side settled on two circular walls with a radius of 34 metres, placed symmetrically either side of the pavilion. The horizontal pressure of the sand, that in places reaches a height of six metres against the wall, is optimally absorbed by these curved walls.

Given the nature of the materials used in some of the sculptures – softwoods and soft stone, textile, plaster of Paris and suchlike – both indoor and outdoor exhibition areas were required. The wall on the north side encloses a large indoor exhibition area and two patios. On the south side are a patio and three ascending terraces for the larger part of the outdoor exhibition. The terraces lie more or less on the surface of the dune while the large indoor area is buried in the body of dune. Between the two areas enclosed by the circle segments, lies the heart of the museum. Here, pavilion and museum form a single entity: the cellars under the main hall of the pavilion were deepened and connected to the museum via three large openings in the walls on the seaward side. The resulting room has an old masonry and vaulted construction which gives it a special character. Originally dubbed the Cellar Room, it is now known as the Wilhelmina Room (Wilhelmina was the name of the queen for whom the pavilion was built and the third given name of Mrs Scholten-Miltenburg). On either side of this room, spaces were created for storage and for the two connecting passages between the north and south sections of the museum. These corridors are also used for exhibitions, for which purpose four semi-circular and two rectangular niches were made in the walls.

On the seaward side of the pavilion is another room: the Sea Room. The dune in front of it has been slightly lowered so that a strip of sea is just visible over the top of the marram grass. The roof of the Sea Room doubles as the enlarged terrace of the pavilion.

Quist wanted to reserve all the spaces inside the circles for exhibitions. Auxiliary spaces – entrance hall and reception desk, café, auditorium, library, toilets and store room – are located in the entrance building, between Harteveltstraat and the indoor exhibition area. Large, two-metre-wide openings in the curved concrete wall link the entrance hall to the exhibition space.

All the museum walls, with the exception of the low partition walls in the entrance building, are executed in *in situ* cast concrete. All the concrete is visible and has received no surface treatment. The choice of fair-faced, off-the-form concrete, had several implications. For example, the six-metre-high walls had to be poured in one go to their full height so as to avoid horizontal construction joints. In fair-faced concrete without surface treatment, the formwork leaves a distinct impression in the surface of the concrete, so the formwork pattern had to be precisely defined in the specifications. All the concrete walls, inside and outside, were cast in plywood form boards, 123 cm wide and 83 cm high, with a form tie in the centre of the board to fix the distance between the two forms. The outer, cone-shaped parts of the form ties are usually twisted out of the concrete after the formwork has been removed. The resulting depressions are then filled up with mortar, but they always leave a mark in surface of the

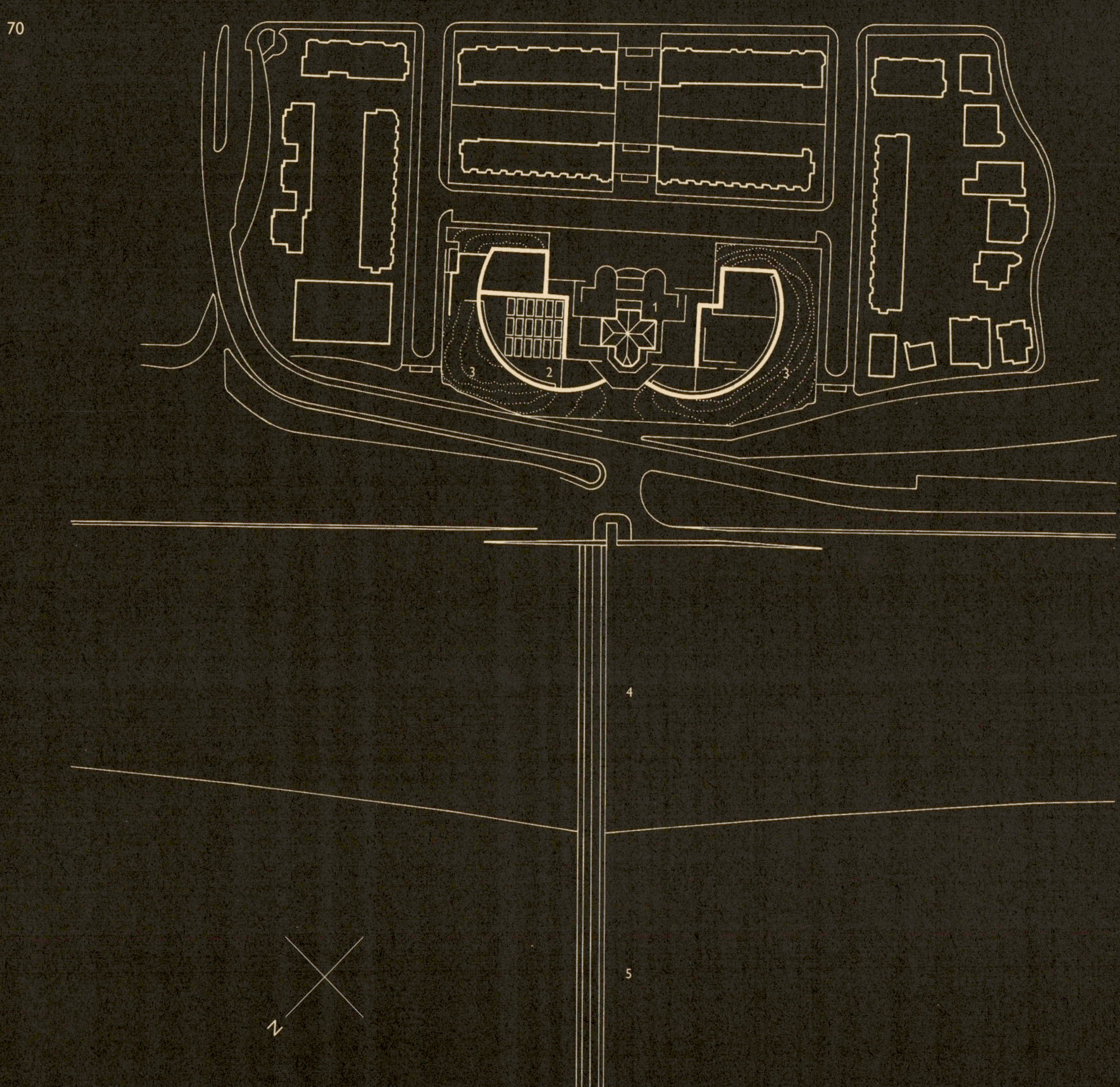

Situation
1 Old pavilion
2 Museum
3 Dune
4 Beach
5 North Sea
70
1
2
3
3
4
5
N

concrete. In Beelden aan Zee, the cones were replaced by permanent stainless steel bushes with a flange and internal screw thread. Each form tie thus constitutes a potential attachment point for a sculpture bracket. Moreover, the regularly spaced steel 'studs' and the consistent formwork pattern combine to give the concrete a very restful appearance. This is further enhanced by the colour of the concrete which was chosen, at the client's request, to blend in with the dune landscape. All the concrete, *in situ* and precast, is tinted a beige-yellow colour.

The sand not only surrounds the museum, but in places covers it. The entrance building, which is buried under a layer of sand up to three metres in depth, was therefore given a bunker-like construction with a concrete roof up to 90 cm thick in places. But there is nothing bunker-like about the roof of the adjacent main exhibition room. Unlike paintings, sculptures can stand any amount of light, including direct sunlight, and this they certainly get. The light enters the room via the roof in two ways: through eighteen individual skylights and through a continuous rooflight along the curved concrete wall. This wall, in order to be able to contain and resist the dune sand outside, had to be some six metres in height. The roof of the room, which did not need to be so high, is one and a half metres lower. Quist bridged this difference in height by introducing a 1.8 metre-wide 'light corridor' between the concrete wall and the roof. The effect of the light thus shed on the curved wall is all the more intriguing because its source is invisible from most parts of the room.

The roof has a simple steel construction of broad-flanged sections for principal and secondary beams laid on round columns, centre to centre, 7.5 metres in both directions. The columns stand only in the 22.5 by 22.5 metre squares formed by the eighteen skylights. The beams at this point are topped with grooves of profiled steel plate on which the skylights rest. The roof is finished with a layer of foamed concrete as added protection against wind and weather. For the same reason, those parts of the steel construction exposed to the outside air have been hot-galvanized; the other parts are painted a light colour.

All the floors are flagged in a consistent pattern of six by six 40 cm tiles within a 10 cm-wide border. Inside, the floors are of sand-coloured granite; outside, concrete flags are set in a granite border. The steps and the ramp are also granite. The tile pattern module, with a centre-to-centre distance of 6 x 40 + 10 = 250 cm, matches the steel construction, as can be clearly seen in the cross-shaped bases of the round columns. The only deviation from this module is the 123 cm of the formwork pattern of the concrete walls.

The ceiling, which consists of American pinewood strips, extends several metres over the aluminium facade sections into the patios.

The dune is now higher than it was originally, owing to the Hoogheemraadschap's demand that most of the sand should remain on the site. The low brick retaining wall that previously enclosed the dune was replaced by a prefab concrete retaining wall over two metres high. Since this wall has a major visual impact on the streets bordering the museum, a good deal of attention was paid to its appearance. The joints and the upper edge have been given an indented profiling and lighting elements have been incorporated into the wall at 7.5 m intervals. The surface of the wall has been treated with an anti-graffiti coating.

Construction

Even after an agreement had been reached with a firm of contractors (Van Splunder's Aannemingsmaatschappij), it was another year before all the appeal proceedings had been completed and all the necessary permits obtained. Construction started in August 1993 and on 9 September 1994 the museum was officially opened by the queen. The project was completed on schedule but it had been no easy task.

Apart from the usual inconveniences associated with building along the coast – constant wind and sand every-

Ground floor
1 Entrance-hall
2 Restaurant
3 Auditorium
4 Library
5 Office
6 Depot
7 Service
8 Exposition
9 Patio
10 Old pavilion

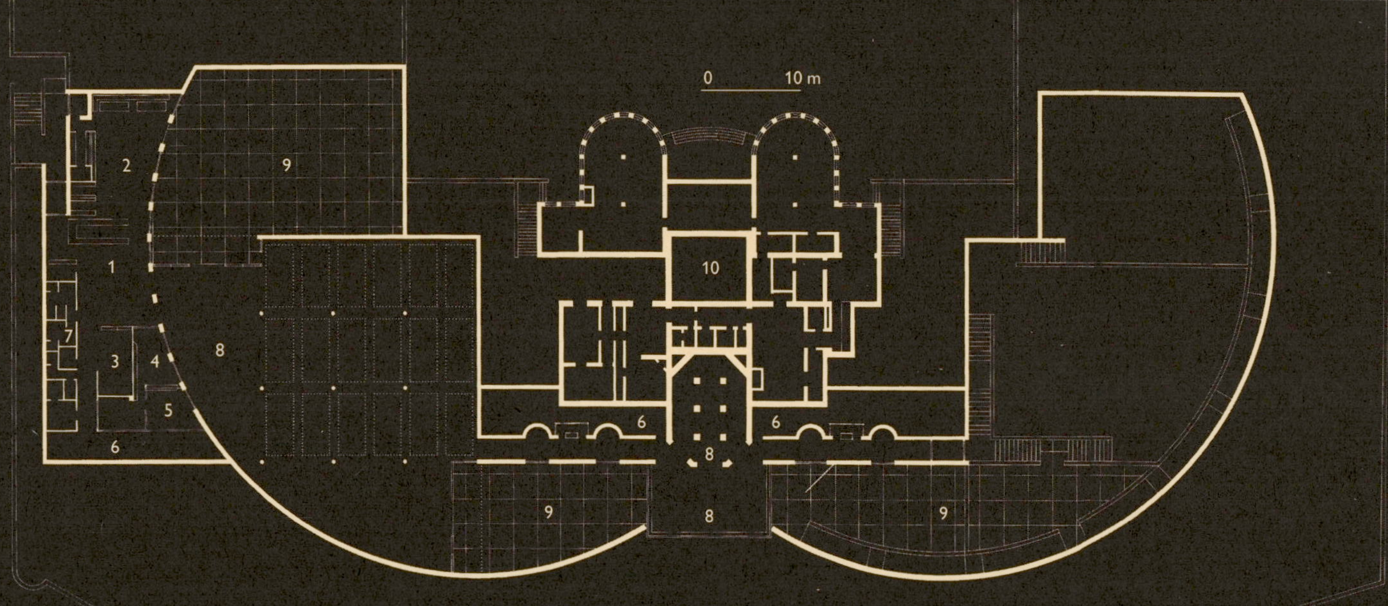

where – the execution also presented a few unique problems.

For instance, the Germans had left behind several wartime structures in the dune, including a bunker with two-metre-thick concrete walls. Unfortunately of excellent quality. As demolition with explosives was ruled out because of the location, it took two months of working with pneumatic hammers to remove the obstacle. This was the first setback.

While excavating the foundations of the large room in the pavilion, the builders met with a second surprise. It had always been assumed that the floor of the Sea Room could without too much difficulty be connected up to the pavilion cellar. They now discovered that the construction level of the cellar foundations was over a metre higher than the level of the museum floor. A solution had to be found and fast. To avoid the risk of deformation and cracking in the pavilion, it was decided to petrify the soil under the high foundation by injecting it with a mixture of hardener and water glass. This increased the strength of the soil so much that it was possible to chip it away a bit at a time and replace it with load bearing masonry. This work was carried out in a number of phases. For a column, for instance, the procedure was as follows: first the soil was chipped away on one side; then a strip of concrete floor was poured on this side; once the concrete had hardened, the masonry wall was laid on top of it. Then the process was repeated on the opposite side of the column and finally, simultaneously on the remaining two sides. In this way, step by step, the bottom metre of masonry was laid for the basement room and the store rooms. All in all, in a short space of time, 150 cubic metres of dune sand was injected with 60,000 litres of injection material.

So much for the unforeseen obstacles encountered during construction. The fact that the rest of the construction had been foreseen does not mean that it was all plain sailing. There was, for instance, the problem of the colour of the concrete. The chosen colour, beige-yellow, the colour of

sand, can be achieved by adding iron oxide to the concrete slurry. But the effect is different in precast concrete than in *in situ* cast concrete, different again in Portland cement than in blast furnace slag cement, and on top of this the colour also changes during the first months after pouring. After a comparison of a great many test pieces, it was decided to use 0.4% pigment in the precast elements and 0.2% in the *in situ* cast concrete. The result is a success; the concrete is the same sand-yellow colour virtually everywhere and on the terraces in particular one can see how well this blends with the dune. Only the concrete slabs are a little greyer but this does not detract from the overall effect.*

The casting of the high walls was no simple matter, especially in those places where the insulation had to be incorporated in the wall. All the walls between indoors and outdoors are insulated. In places where one side of the wall remains hidden from view, the insulation has been stuck to the surface of the concrete; where both sides of the concrete are permanently visible or likely to become visible, such as the top metre of the retaining wall, the insulation has been incorporated into the 40 cm-thick wall. A 5 cm-thick sheet of insulating material leaves 15 to 20 cm on either side. In coastal regions, concrete needs to have a compact structure. This means a concrete slurry with little mixing water and consequently difficult to pour, certainly through a slot 5 to 6 metres high and 15 to 20 cm wide. All the imperfections that came to light after the stripping of the form received a cosmetic treatment which consisted of carefully sponging down the surface with an appropriately coloured mortar.

One construction joint stands out. At a late stage in the execution, the already finished wall between the large patio and the car park was raised by two metres in order to reinforce the enclosed character of the museum. The result is a distinct seam at a height of two metres and a rather odd looking door with flap. It is not the museum's finest wall. But the fact that the problems associated with

South side

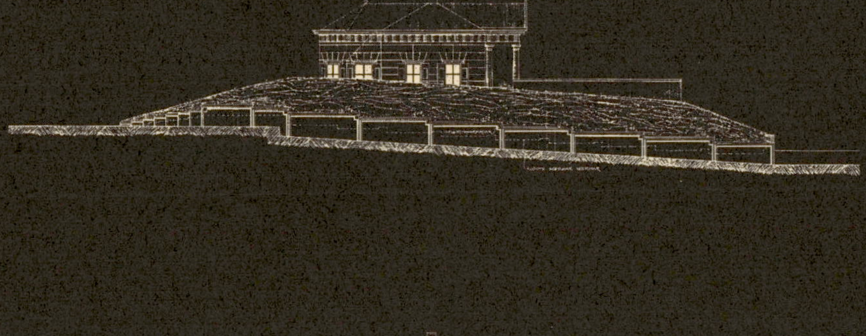

North side

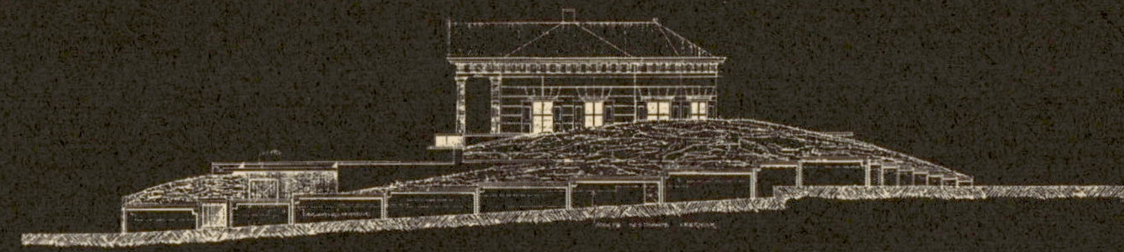

West side

the construction have left no other traces, must be counted
a success for all involved.

Result

The result is a dune that harbours a splendid museum.
On the dune there is still only one building, the pavilion, as
stipulated by the client. Nearly all the dune sand has been
retained on the site, as demanded by the Hoogheemraadschap.

By integrating the dune and the museum, Quist has
managed to exploit the limitations of the site to generate
an additional quality. The visitor enters not just a museum,
but also a dune. This is already apparent at the entrance on
Harteveltstraat: it is the entrance to a dune, an interruption
of the precast retaining wall, hardly more noticeable than
the rabbit hole by which Alice entered her Wonderland.
Stairs or a wheelchair lift bring visitors into the entrance
building from where they can also see the main exhibition
room and the large patio. From the skylights and the rooflight along the curved wall, the room is flooded with light.
Because of this and the light-coloured walls and floor, no
one is conscious of the metres of sand behind the wall and
on top of the entrance building.

The sand and a narrow strip of sea only come into view
when one reaches the Sea Room. In fact there is very little
sea to be seen, but a finer seascape than here, above a
recumbent Venus by Meefout, would be difficult to find.
Behind the Sea Room, the Wilhelmina Room with its
masonry vaults forms as it were the interface with the old
pavilion, four metres higher.

On the south side, the curved wall escorts a ramp to the
ascending terraces which seem to have merged naturally
with the dune even though the highest one, the panorama
terrace, lies several metres higher than the original dune.
But precisely because of this, it offers a magnificent view of
the sea, far removed from the boulevard culture, and of the
sculptures in the outdoor exhibition.

As such, the museum has been inserted very naturally
into and on top of the dune and the dune has been slightly
adapted to accommodate the museum. It all seems very
logical and obvious. The same is true of the design of the
component parts: the curved walls like two circles, the
simple entrance, the 'light corridor' between wall and
roof, the choice of visual concrete and its colour, and even
such details as the modified form ties. It is all so straight-
forward and in fact self-evident that everyone is able to
say: that's how I would have done it too. That is what is
unique about Quist's design.

Wim van der Vlugt

R. Nijsse of ABT Adviesbureau voor Bouwtechniek in Velp provided a lot of information for
this text.

* More detailed information about the concrete composition can be found in: R. Nijsse et al.,
'Museum Beelden aan Zee te Scheveningen', *Cement* 1994 no. 11.

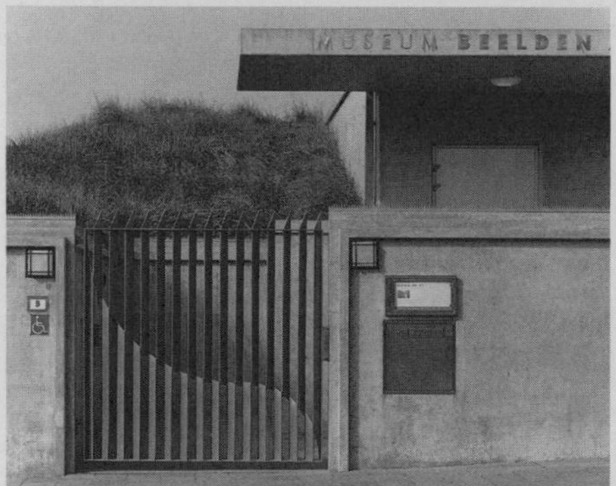

Entrance gate, design André Volten

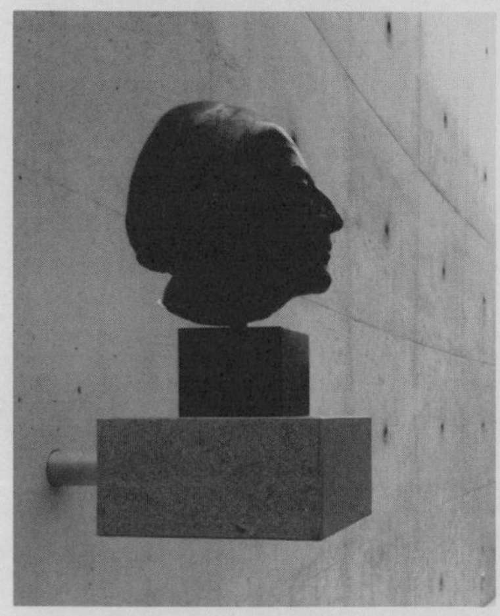

Display bracket attachment, design Willem Lenssinck

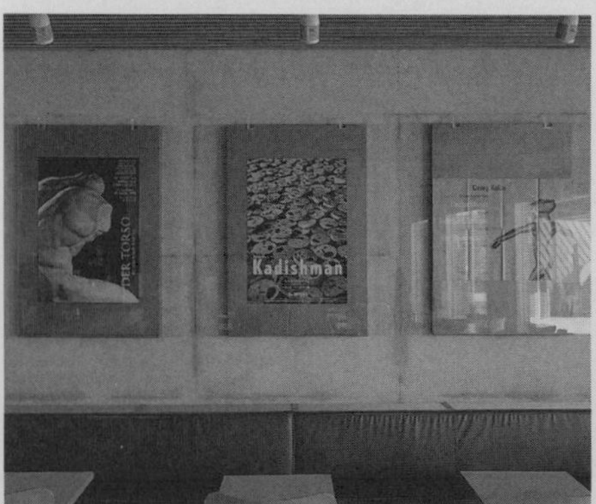

Sponsor and poster boards, design Willem Lenssinck

Client
Stichting 'De Onvoltooide'
Architect
Wim Quist, Rotterdam
Consultant
ABT Adviesbureau voor Bouwtechniek, Velp
Contractor
Van Splunder's Aannemingsmaatschappij, Ridderkerk
Construction started
August 1993
Opening
9 September 1994 by Her Majesty, Queen Beatrix
Indoor exhibition
1100 m²
Outdoor exhibition
2000 m²
Other spaces
700 m²

Several artists contributed to the building. André Volten designed the gate at the entrance and Willem Lenssinck made the sponsor and poster boards. Lensinck also devised the system for attaching display brackets using the stainless steel flanges that are a feature of the museum walls.

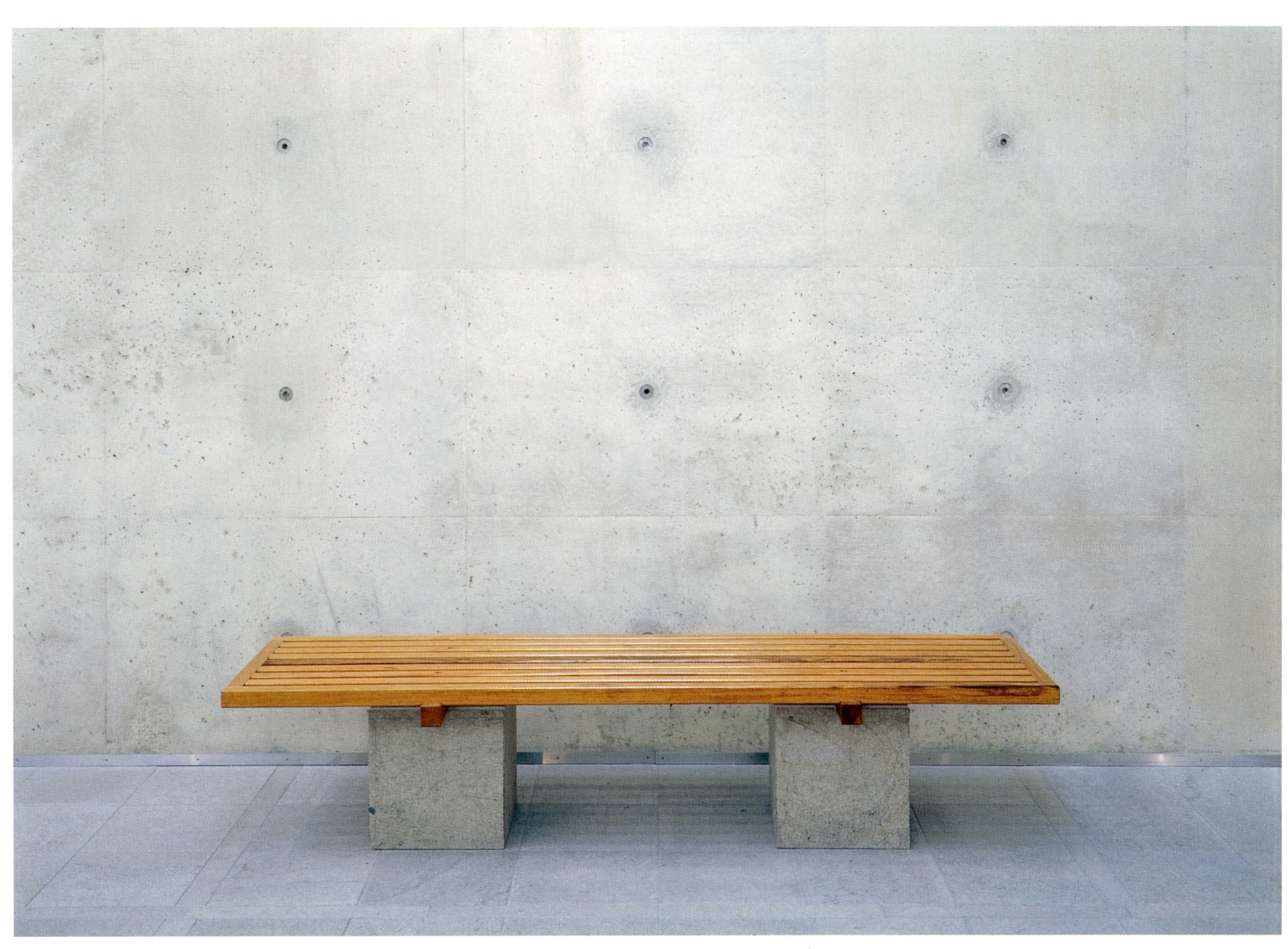

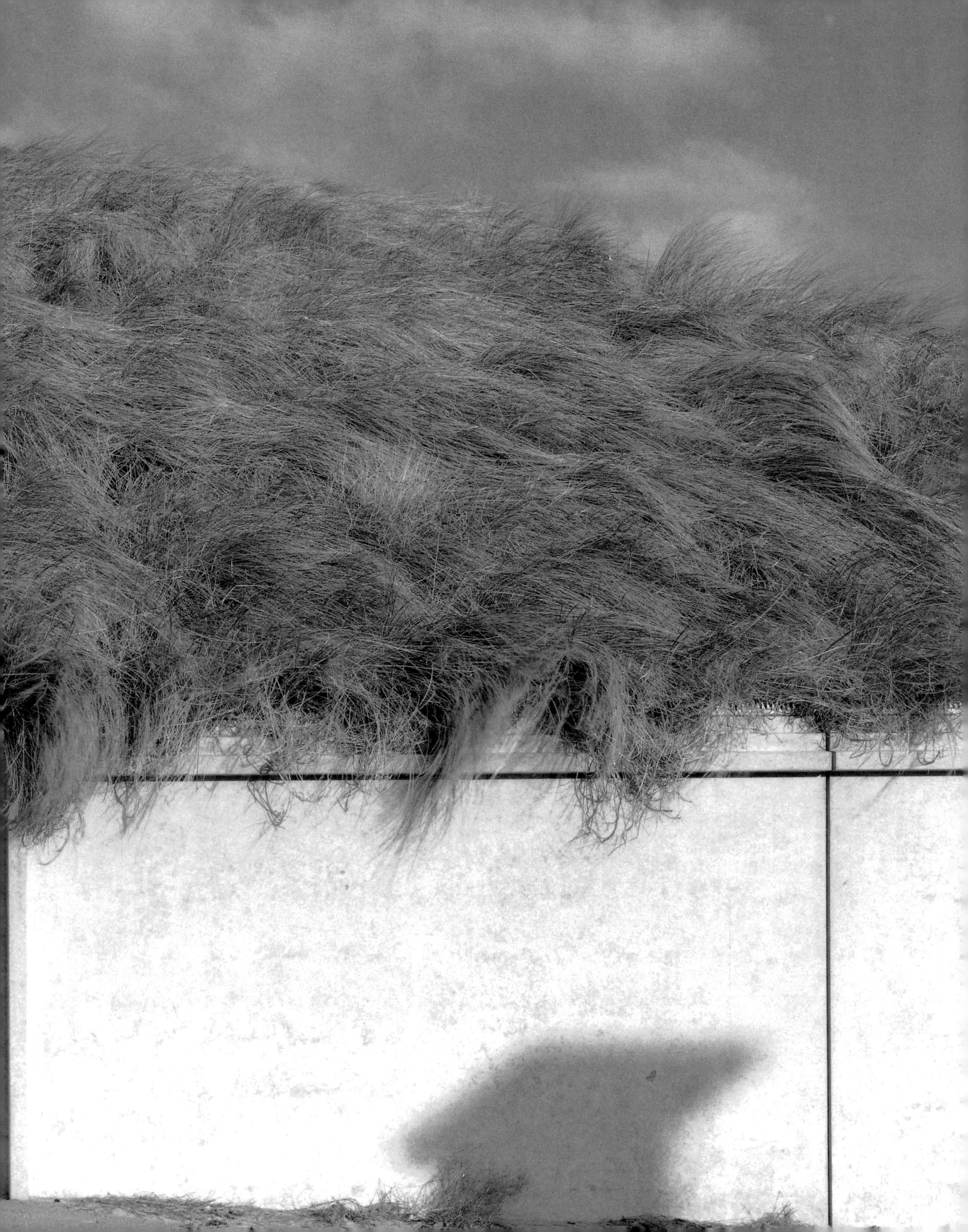

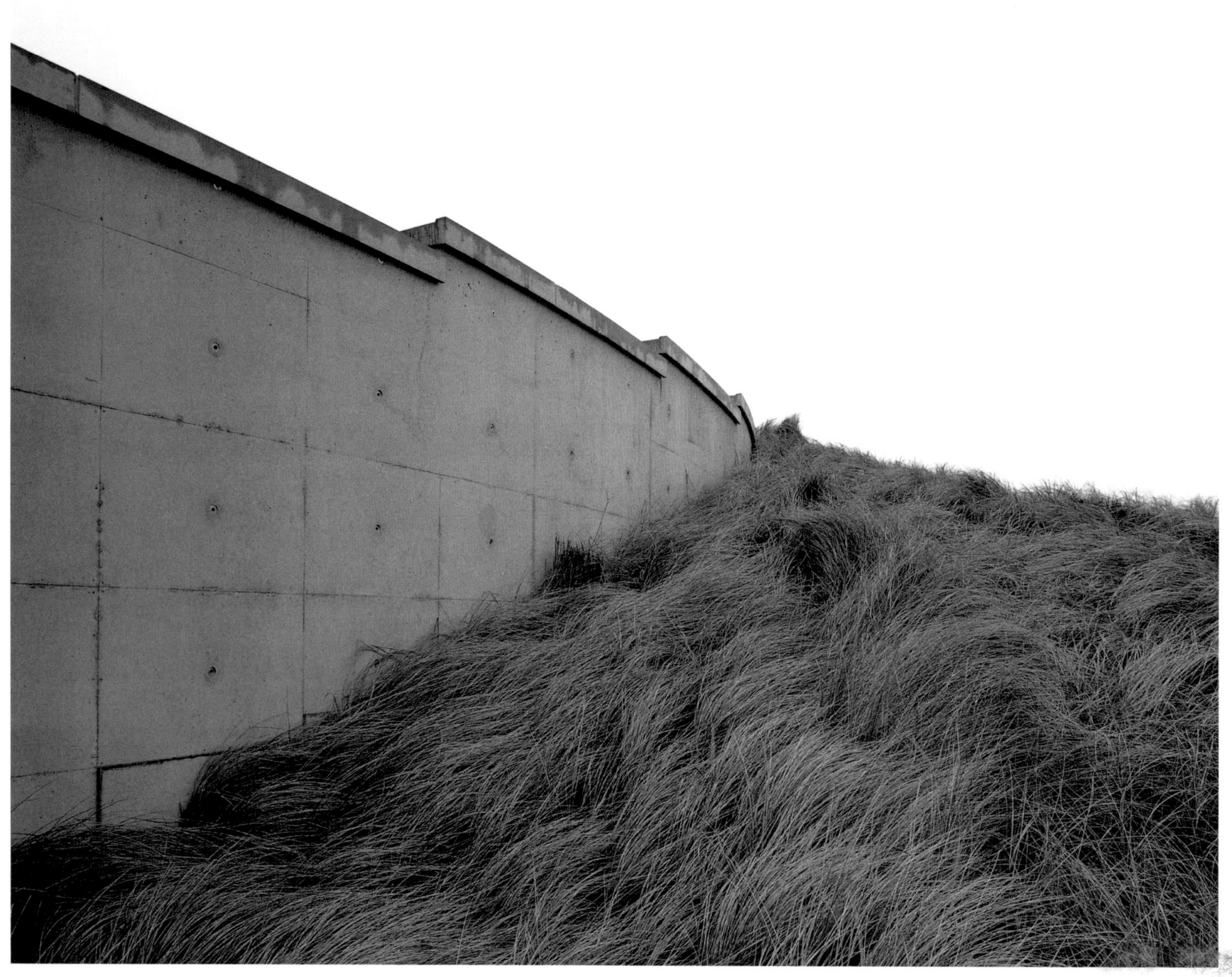

Documentation

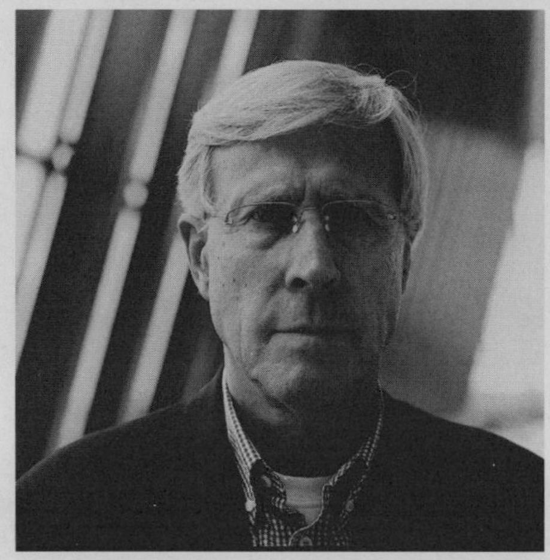

1930
Born in Amsterdam
1958
Wins the Prix de Rome silver medal
1960
Graduates from the Academy of Architecture, Amsterdam
Sets up office in Rotterdam
1968-1975
Professor of architectural and urban design at Eindhoven
Technical College
1970
Member of judges' panel (Staatsprijs voor Architectuur).
Receives the A.J. van Eck Prize for the Berenplaat waterpurification
plant.
1975-1980
Rijksbouwmeester ('State Architect')
1977
Member of judges' panel (National Gallery, Toronto, Canada)
1978
Member of panel judging the competition for extentions to Parliament,
The Hague
1979
Member of judges' panel (David Roëll Prize)
1980
Member of judges' panel (Rotterdam Maaskant-Prize)
Awarded the Nationale Staalprijs for the German-Dutch wind tunnel
with Adviesbureau A.B.T., Arnhem
1982
Member of judges' panel (Prix de Rome)
1982-
Member of the Board of Rotterdam Fine Arts Academy
1983
Awarded the Nationale Staalprijs (honorary mention) for Van der
Giessen-De Noord shipbuilders' shed with Adviesbureau Aronsohn,
(Rotterdam)
1984
Takes part in 'Kunst uit Rotterdam', exhibition in Boymans-van Beuningen
Museum, Rotterdam
'Quist, architect, 20 jaar activiteit', exhibition in Noordbrabants
Museum, Den Bosch
1985
Member of judges' panel (Erasmus Prize)
Receives the Betonprijs for the Oosterschelde flood control building,
together with the Ministry of Works (Rijkswaterstaat)

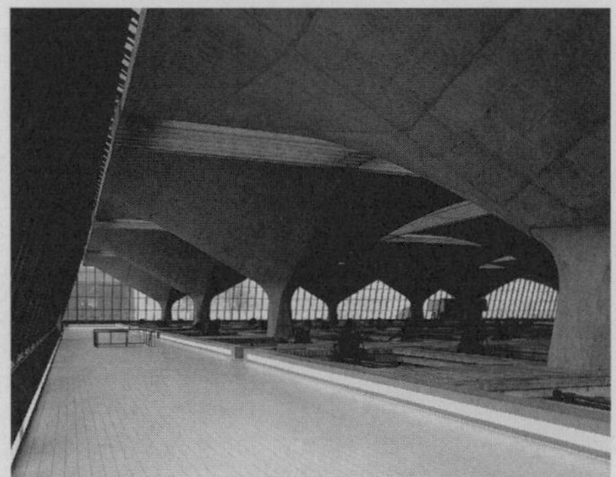

Waterpurification plant Berenplaat, Oud-Beijerland

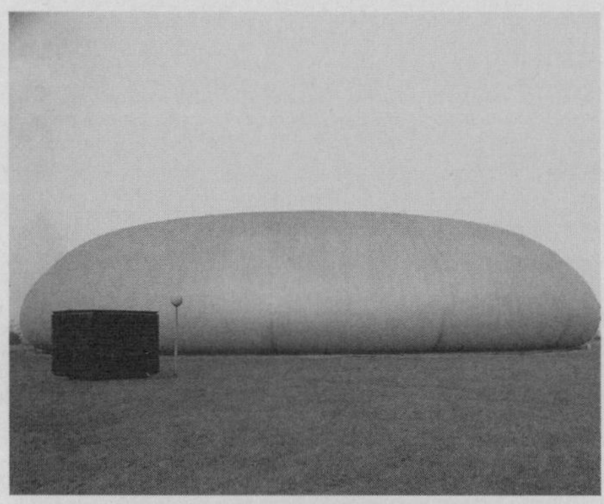

Waterpurification plant Kralingen, Rotterdam

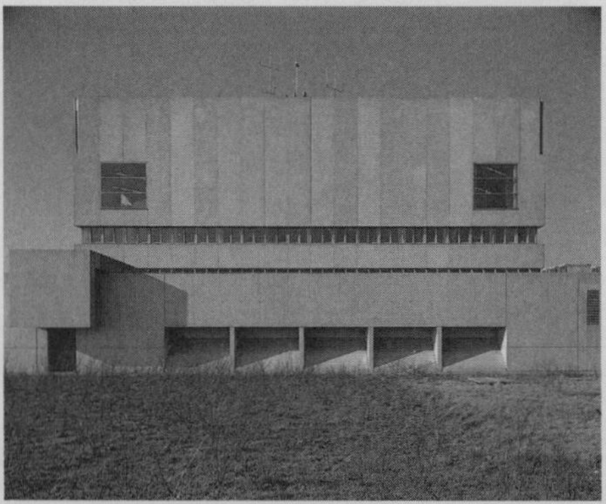

Service Building Oosterschelde Flood Barrier, Neeltje Jans

1985-
Member of the advisory committee of Boymans-van Beuningen
Museum, Rotterdam
1985-
Member of general committee to Stichting Praemium Erasmianum,
Amsterdam
1986
Receives Dutch Architects' Association 'kubus' award for his
complete works
1987
Awarded the Betonprijs for the architectural design of the Oosterschelde
flood barrier together with the Ministry of Works (Rijkswaterstaat)
Awarded the Cultuurprijs by the Province of Zuid-Holland
Extraordinary professor of architectural design for Amsterdam College
of the Arts at the Language Faculty of Amsterdam University
1987-1989
Member of the Municipal Historic Buildings Committee
(Monumentencommissie), Dordrecht
1989
Awarded the David Roëll Prize for his complete work

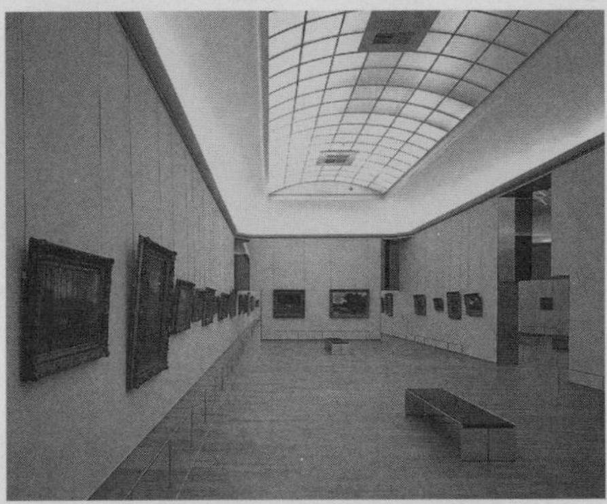
Extension to Rijksmuseum Kröller-Müller, Otterlo

Renovation of Zuidvleugel Rijksmuseum, Amsterdam

Renovation of Rijksmuseum, Amsterdam

Texts by Wim Quist

– 'The yoke is sweet', inaugural lecture Technische Hogeschool
Eindhoven 13 June 1969
– 'Creativiteit', lecture held in 1973, *De raadgevende ingenieur* 1974 no. 1
– Bureau Rijksbouwmeester, *Jaarverslag Rijksgebouwendienst,* The Hague
1975, 73-74
– 'Over de noodzaak van beleid', valedictory lecture Technische Hoge-
school Eindhoven 14 March 1975
– 'Van beslissen naar bijsturen', *Bouw* 1975 no. 18, 361-362
– Bureau Rijksbouwmeester, *Jaarverslag Rijksgebouwendienst,* The Hague
1976, 61-65
– 'Zuivere integratie van constructie in de architectuur', *Plan* 1976 no. 4,
71-75
– Bureau Rijksbouwmeester, *Jaarverslag Rijksgebouwendienst,* The Hague
1977, 94-99
– Bureau Rijksbouwmeester, *Jaarverslag Rijksgebouwendienst,* The Hague
1978, 120-126
– 'Natuurlijkheid gepaard aan distinctie', *Plan* 1979 no. 11, 16-25
– 'Verstaanbaarheid', *Plan* 1982 no. 9, 38-41
– 'Pieter Saenredam', opening address 'Perspectieven' exhibition,
Museum Boymans-van Beuningen, Rotterdam 1991
– *G. Rietveld, erflater van de twintigste eeuw,* Querido 1991
– 'Gebouwen voor cultuur, voor schoonheid en contemplatie', speech at
symposium held to mark his departure as architect for the Rijksmuseum,
Amsterdam 1996

Interviews with Wim Quist

– Roos, J., 'Praten met Wim Quist, de rijksbouwmeester', *Het Parool*
18 February 1977
– Jippes, H., 'Hoe ontwerp je een nieuwe gevangenis? Rijksbouwmeester
Quist: inspraak gevangenen', *Het Parool* 20 March 1979
– Haan, H. de, I. Haagsma, 'W.G. Quist: :"Het gaat erom de essentie van
de opgave te vinden"', *Intermediair* 1979 no. 45, 13-17
– Brouwers, R., 'Wim Quist vertrekt als rijksbouwmeester met een
zeker cynisme: "Bij architecten en hun critici heerst gebrek aan scherpe
analyse"', *Wonen-TABK* 1979 no. 23, 9-12
– Dijk, H. van, 'Gesloten dozen vol emoties', *NRC Handelsblad,* 2 March
1984
– Kroon, B. (ed.), 'Zulk grijs kunnen alleen schilders maken', *De Tijd,*
22 June 1984
– 'In gesprek met Wim G. Quist', *Bulletin van het Rijksmuseum* 1 985 no.
3, 160-175
– Linden, F. van der, 'Het gebouw heeft altijd gelijk', *De Tijd,* 15 March 1985

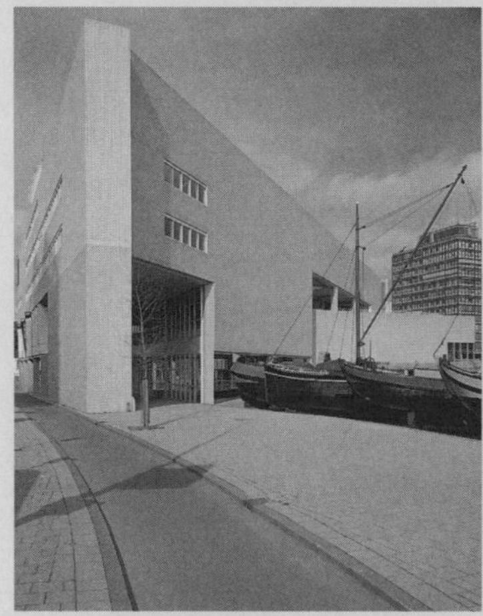

Maritime Museum 'Prins Hendrik', Rotterdam

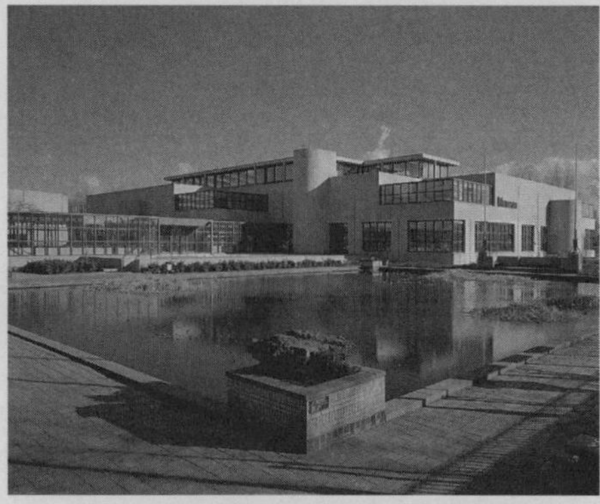

Museon and Omniversum, The Hague

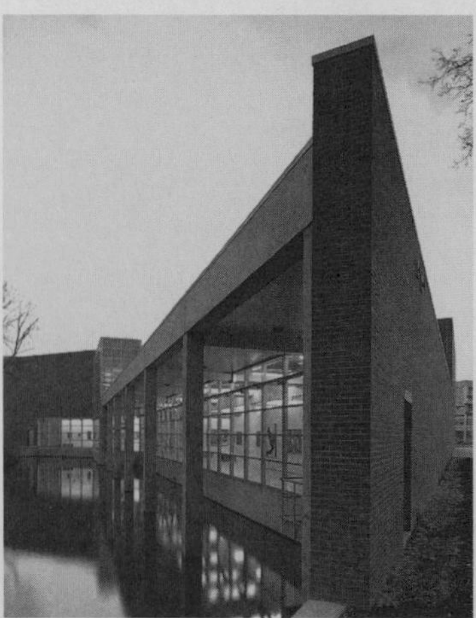

Cobra Museum for Modern Art, Amstelveen

– Beek, M. van, 'Het dramatiseren van een situatie', *Kunstbeeld* 1987 no. 2, 42-47
– Casciato, M., 'Zeven vragen over het ontwerpen en gebruiken van een museum', in: P. Cavalcanti, *Musea van moderne kunst in Nederland*, Rome 1987
– Wesseling, J. 'Architecten kiezen kunst', *Kwartaalblad Kunst en Bedrijf* vol. 3 no. 1, March 1989

Articles about Wim Quist

– Couwelaar, W.R. van, 'Over onbehagen', *Futura* 1979 no. 10, 8-11; no. 12, 6-11
– Barbieri, U., 'De nieuwe truttigheid is dood, wat nu?', *Plan* 1979 no. 11, 40-47
– Daru, M., 'Bouwen of architectuur?', *Plan* 1980 no. 2, 25-26
– Struijs, M., 'Noodzaak van een theorie', *Plan* 1982 no. 2, 25-26
– Dijk, H. van, 'De uitdaging van het onmogelijke. Paradoxen in woorden en werken van W.G. Quist', *Wonen-TABK* 1984 no. 3, 8-28
– Kloos, M., 'Soms monumentale allure, dan weer naakte waarheid, Architect Quist is een romanticus met een voorliefde voor eenvoud', *de Volkskrant* 30 March 1984
– Buchanan, R., 'Rotterdam Rationalists', *Architectural Review* 1985 no. 1, 39-41
– Lootsma, B., M. Steigenga, 'Ontwerpen met de ogen dicht: architectuur van het ik-tijdperk', *Forum* 1986 no. 1, 28-35
– Huisman, J., 'De sobere maat van de zee, Wim Quist: poëzie en muziek zeggen meer over de samenleving dan architectuur', *de Volkskrant* 15 April 1988
– Metz, T., H. Nijenhuis, 'Architect met hart van kunstenaar, Wim G. Quist, in vrijheid kiezen voor begrenzing', *NRC Handelsblad* 24 May 1988

Books

Wim Quist Architect, [Dutch/English] Uitgeverij 010, Rotterdam 1989
Wim Quist Projecten 87-92, Uitgeverij 010, Rotterdam 1992

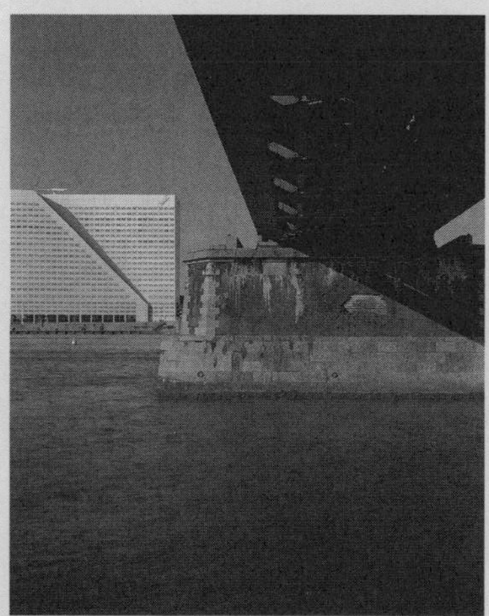
Willemswerf office building, Rotterdam

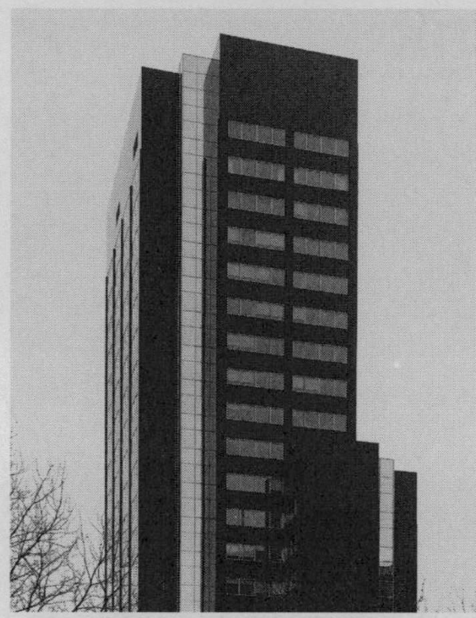
Robeco office building, Rotterdam

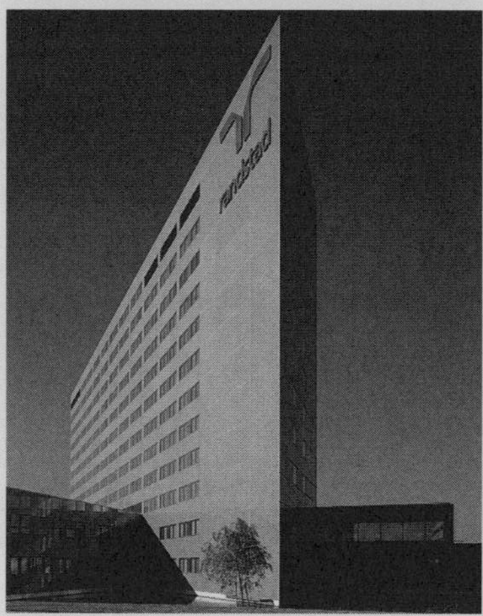
Randstad office building, Diemen

Projects by Wim Quist

1959-1965
Berenplaat Waterworks, Oud-Beijerland
1968-1970
Watertower, Eindhoven
1970-1977
Extension to Rijksmuseum Kröller-Müller, Otterlo
1973-1977
Kralingen Waterworks, Rotterdam
1977-1985
Museon and Omniversum, The Hague
1980-1986
Service Building Oosterschelde Flood Barrier, Neeltje Jans
1981-1986
Maritime Museum 'Prins Hendrik', Rotterdam
1981-1990
Renovation Rijksmuseum, Amsterdam
1982-1988
Willemswerf office building, Rotterdam
1982-1988
City Theatre, Rotterdam
1982-1987
Extension and renovation of Noordbrabants Museum, 's-Hertogenbosch
1987-1990
Randstad office building, Diemen
1987-1991
Robeco office building, Rotterdam
1987-1991
Extension to Erasmus Universiteit, Rotterdam
1992-1995
Cobra Museum for Modern Art, Amstelveen
1992-1996
South Wing renovation at Rijksmuseum, Amsterdam
1995-1997
Town Hall, Bodegraven
1995-1997
Head Office Schiphol Airport

Notes on contributors

Rutger Kopland (1934, Goor) is the pseudonym of Dr R.H. van den Hoofdakker, Professor Emeritus of Biological Psychiatry at Groningen University. In addition to many scholarly articles on psychiatry, he has published eleven volumes of poetry and many essays. His first volume of poems was *Onder het vee* (1966), his latest, *Tot het ons loslaat* (1997); his collections of essays include *Het mechaniek van de ontroering* (1994) and *Mooi, maar dat is het woord niet* (1998). (All published by Van Oorschot.) Over the years Rutger Kopland has won many literary prizes: in 1970 the Jan Campert prize, in 1975 the Herman Gorter prize, in 1982 the Paul Snoek prize, in 1988 the P.C. Hooft prize and in 1998 the VSB poetry prize.

Fons Asselbergs (1940, Amsterdam) is an architectural historian. After grammar school he went on to study art history at Nijmegen. From 1971 to 1978 he was custodian of the Netherlands Architectural Documentation Centre in Amsterdam. From 1978 to 1993 he was an alderman in Amersfoort. It was during this period that the historic town centre of Amersfoort was restored and the celebrated Kattenbroek housing estate was built. Since 1993 he has been director of the Department for the Conservation of Historic Buildings and Sites where he has widened the preservation of monuments to include preservation of the surrounding area. Fons Asselbergs has occupied and still occupies many other positions in field of spatial planning, architectural policy and preservation.

Ole Bouman (1960, Amersfoort) combined two areas of study at the University of Amsterdam, crowning both with a single MA thesis: History and Art History & Archeology (cum laude). He has published a number of books, and many articles in both Dutch and foreign journals, in particular on architecture. Until recently he wrote a fortnightly column in the *De Groene Amsterdammer*. He has organized conferences and exhibitions, and fills various advisory and administrative positions. Ole Bouman is currently editor of the noted Dutch architectural journal *Archis*.

Joost van der Grinten (1927, Venlo) grew up in a musical family where he developed an early interest in making models and instruments; he made his first violin at the age of fifteen. After studying architecture at Delft, he set up his own practice and in 1954 won the Prix de Rome for architecture. He has built offices, factories, churches and houses. In addition to his architectural work, he was professor of Industrial Design at Delft University of Technology. In 1970, at the age of 43, he bid farewell to his successful but exhausting architectural career and returned to the love of his youth: violin making. He set himself to learn a new craft and over the next 25 years he built and restored numerous instruments. His wife, Trip van der Grinten, took care of the correspondence and administration of what has since become the 'family business': three of their four children have opted for the world of the violin.

Theo Scholten (1927, Spanbroek) grew up in a large family where music, and especially singing, played an important role. He was a boy soprano and later studied for several years at the Royal Conservatory in The Hague. He completed advanced elementary education and went to work at the age of fifteen. In the evenings he studied; first for university entrance exam and then Economy at Rotterdam, graduating cum laude in 1962. He has a long history of involvement in church and social work. He has worked in business, most recently as chairman of the board of the Robeco Group. From 1971 to 1992 he was professor at the Erasmus University in Rotterdam. He holds administrative and advisory functions in both the business and art worlds. Mr and Mrs Scholten have been collecting sculpture for over thirty years and in 1994 they founded the Beelden aan Zee Museum to house their collection; both have been awarded the Zilveren Anjer in recognition of their services to art.

Wim van der Vlugt (1923, Heemstede) attended grammar school in Haarlem before going on to study civil engineering at Delft. For many years he was professionally involved in the application of prestressed concrete, a French invention, in civil engineering structures. He worked, for instance, on a suspension bridge over the Seine, the drainage sluices in Haringvliet and the viaducts of the bridge over the Bosporus near Istanbul. From 1969 to 1988 he was professor of Structural Design at Eindhoven University of Technology where he also for many years held administrative positions within the Faculty of Architecture. He has held several other administrative functions, has acted as arbitrator and has been editor of the journal *Cement*.

Kim Zwarts (1955, Maastricht) received his training at the Academy of Applied Arts in Maastricht. He has worked as photographer on many architectural books, including publications devoted to the work of Wim Quist, Wiel Arets, Dom van der Laan, Charles Vandenhove and Morphosis. He has also taken part in photographic projects in the Netherlands and elsewhere. Exhibitions of his work have been held in the Bonnefantenmuseum in Maastricht, the Nederlands Foto Instituut in Rotterdam, the Berlage Instituut in Amsterdam and at the Biennale de la Photographie et des Arts Visuels in Liège. In 1989 he received the Kodak Award and in 1997 the Werner Mantz Prize.

Reynoud Homan (1956, Eindhoven) studied graphic design and typography at the Koninklijke Academie van Beeldende Kunsten in The Hague and at Reading University (England). Since 1986 he has worked as a freelance designer. Book design is his most important activity and his projects in this area include a sixteen-part monograph series on Dutch architects (the first part of which is devoted to the work of Wim Quist). He designs publications for a wide range of clients such as museums, artists and photographers. Several of his book designs have won prizes, both in the Netherlands and abroad. He also teaches at the Gerrit Rietveld Academy in Amsterdam.

Colophon

This book has been made possible by a grant from the Netherlands Architecture Fund, Rotterdam; we would also like to express our gratitude for support received from ABT Adviesbureau.

Concept
Theo Scholten

Editor
Karel Jongtien

Translation
James Brockway (Rutger Kopland), Robyn de Jong-Dalziel

Photography
Kim Zwarts

Design
Reynoud Homan

Printing
Drukkerij Rosbeek bv

Production
Els Brinkman

Publisher
Simon Franke

Available in North, South and Central America through D.A.P./Distributed Art Publishers Inc, 155 Sixth Avenue 2nd Floor, New York, NY 10013-1507, T 212 627.1999 F 212 627.9484

ISBN 90-5662-097-5